# THE SHOOTING SCRIPT®
# A BEAUTIFUL MIND

D1344906

# A BEAUTIFUL MIND

### SCREENPLAY AND INTRODUCTION BY
## AKIVA GOLDSMAN

NHB Shooting Scripts
NICK HERN BOOKS • LONDON
www.nickhernbooks.co.uk

Design and compilation copyright © 2002 by Newmarket Press. All rights reserved.

Text and illustrations copyright © 2002 by Universal Studios and DreamWorks LLC. All rights reserved.

This book first published in Great Britain in 2002 as an original paperback
by Nick Hern Books Ltd, The Glasshouse, 49A Goldhawk Road, London W12 8QP,
by arrangement with Newmarket Press, New York.

A CIP catalogue record of this book is available from the British Library.

ISBN 1-85459-681-0

Manufactured in the United States of America.

THE NHB SHOOTING SCRIPT SERIES

*A Beautiful Mind*
*Erin Brockovich*
*I Went Down*
*The Ice Storm*
*Saltwater*
*The Shawshank Redemption*
*The Truman Show*

For information on forthcoming titles, please contact the publisher:
Nick Hern Books, The Glasshouse, 49A Goldhawk Road, London W12 8QP
e-mail: info@nickhernbooks.demon.co.uk

# CONTENTS

**AKIVA GOLDSMAN**'s first screenplay, *Silent Fall,* was filmed by Bruce Beresford. His writing credits include *The Client, Batman Forever, A Time to Kill, Batman and Robin, Lost in Space,* and *Practical Magic.* He is currently adapting *Memoirs of a Geisha* for director Steven Spielberg. Born in Brooklyn Heights, New York, Goldsman received his bachelor's degree from Wesleyan University and attended the graduate writing program at New York University.

# INTRODUCTION

## BY AKIVA GOLDSMAN

I was lucky enough to read Sylvia Nasar's brilliant biography, *A Beautiful Mind*, in galleys. I was instantly mesmerized by John Nash—his genius, his struggle with mental illness, and his triumph.

My interest in the more shadowy corners of the human mind dates back to before I could write—before I could talk, actually. You see, one of the very first group homes for emotionally disturbed children (to use the jargon of the day) was in my house. My parents founded it.

My mother, a gifted child psychologist named Mira Rothenberg, is also a writer. When she writes of those early days in Brooklyn, someone is always bouncing the baby against the wall or hanging the baby out the window. I was the baby.

Many of the children I lived with were diagnosed with childhood schizophrenia. They were labeled as mad, described as being without reason. I am no expert on mental illness, but I am sure of one thing: the children who shared my home were not without reason. Their behavior made sense to them. They had reasons for everything they did. We just couldn't understand their reasons.

So, the idea of writing a screenplay about John's life and the way he saw the world was tremendously exciting to me.

Producer Brian Grazer had also read the book, and Universal Pictures Chairman Stacy Snider had already bought it for Brian's company, Imagine Entertainment. Besides having produced some of the most popular movies of all time, Brian is also known in the film industry as someone who has a longtime fascination with genius.

I asked my agents at Creative Artists Agency for a meeting with Brian. During our meeting, I begged him to hire me—honest, I begged. Because even though I loved this biography, I didn't envision a typical biopic for the story of John Nash.

What intrigued me was a movie inspired by the life of John Nash. A movie built on the natural architecture of his story—Genius, Madness, Nobel Prize. But I also wanted to take some literary license. I wanted to devise a screenplay that evoked the experience of John's journey without attempting a literal depiction of his life. I wanted to take a run at the spirit of John's life, but not just by way of the facts.

Amazingly, Brian didn't throw me out of his office. Instead we got talking about how John's story had moved and inspired him. We got excited, moved our hands a lot when we talked, and scribbled little diagrammatic doodles on paper with labels like "Madness," "Genius," and, oddly, "Beer." And by the end he'd actually hired me to write the screenplay you have in your hand.

I spent several days throwing ideas around with the brilliant Karen Kehela who is Co-Chairman of Imagine Films. Then I drove over to Brian's house early one morning (good house, big). I pitched the story to Brian over coffee. Brian cried (good reaction, big).

I'll skip the writing part, except to say, I used about a million packs of cigarettes, a thousand pots of coffee, several hundred cans of tuna eaten over the sink, and my whole heart.

Then Ron Howard sparked to my first draft and signed on to direct. You know Ron Howard—the man behind *Apollo 13*, *Splash*, *Cocoon*, *Ransom*, and *Parenthood*. So talented with story and gifted with performance that he stands out as one of our greatest filmmakers. That rarest kind of director, relentlessly thorough and startlingly brave. Let me tell you the part you don't know.

Ron Howard is one of my favorite people. What you see is what you get. Turns out he is one of the great guys on the planet. If you have written something you love and you want to give it to someone who will take care of it and make it better than it ever was, give it to Ron Howard.

Next Russell Crowe signed on to play John Nash. Now, Russell Crowe is a genius—an actual one. He not only inhabited the character of John Nash, he re-invented him. With only flesh and emotion as conjuring tools, Russell transformed himself into another being. There are no words to describe watching Russell work. It's watching the most impossible magic show and knowing there are no strings or mirrors. It's watching the real thing.

One of Ron's many notable gifts as a director is his affinity for attracting great actors for his films. The supporting cast for *A Beautiful Mind* still amazes me: Christopher Plummer, Ed Harris, the extraordinary Paul Bettany, and the sublime Jennifer Connelly. How could it get any better?

If you like the screenplay of *A Beautiful Mind*, that's a testament to John and Alicia Nash and how much they inspired all of us.

If it's dedicated to anyone, it's dedicated to anyone anywhere who has ever been told they are insane—told they are without reason—and known better.

Imagine Entertainment's *A Beautiful Mind* is a Universal Pictures and DreamWorks Pictures co-production. Directed by Ron Howard, produced by Brian Grazer and written by Akiva Goldsman, the film stars Oscar® winner Russell Crowe (*Gladiator*), Oscar® nominee Ed Harris (*Pollock, Apollo 13*), and Jennifer Connelly (*Requiem For A Dream*). The cast also includes Paul Bettany (*A Knight's Tale*), Adam Goldberg (*Saving Private Ryan*), Judd Hirsch (*Running on Empty*), Josh Lucas (*You Can Count on Me*), Anthony Rapp (*Road Trip*), newcomer Vivien Cardone, and Christopher Plummer (*The Insider*).

The production team includes director of photography Roger Deakins (Oscar®-nominated for *O Brother, Where Art Thou?*), production designer Wynn Thomas (*Analyze This*), editors Dan Hanley and Mike Hill, winners of the Academy Award® for Best Editing for their work on Ron Howard and Brian Grazer's *Apollo 13*, costume designer Rita Ryack (Oscar®-nominated for *Dr. Seuss' How the Grinch Stole Christmas*), and composer James Horner (an Oscar® winner for *Titanic*). The film's executive producers are Karen Kehela (*Nutty Professor II: The Klumps*) and Todd Hallowell (*The Grinch*).

# A BEAUTIFUL MIND

**written by Akiva Goldsman**

inspired by the life of John Forbes Nash
and
the biography by Sylvia Nasar

Final Shooting Script
June 25, 2001

FADE IN ON:

A STAINED GLASS WINDOW-CLOSE. Sunlight illuminates a complex
pattern of symbols and lines. PULL BACK TO REVEAL...

EXT.-PRINCETON UNIVERSITY-PRESIDENT'S RECEPTION-1947

Students in formal dress mill. An uncommonly handsome man stands
at the bar, gazing up at the window geometry. This is JOHN NASH.

Nash glances down. The light refracting through his glass draws
shifting angles of rainbow on the bar before him.

                    AINSLEY (OVER)
               Hansen's gonna get the brass ring if it
               kills him.

Two more students approach the bar. BENDER is wiry, like a
scarecrow made of skin. AINSLEY is older, sporting the world's
worst tie.

                    BENDER
               He's used to pretty metal.
                    (taps his teeth)
               Silver spoon.

Nash spots the subject of their musings. A dapper student with
fiercely intelligent eyes is pumping hands. MARTIN HANSEN.

                    AINSLEY
               It's not enough he won the Carnegie
               scholarship.

                    BENDER
               He has to have it all for himself.

Hansen and Bender approach the punch bowl.

                    BENDER (CONT'D)
               First time the Carnegie prize has been
               split. Now, Hansen's all bent.

*Nash's gaze drifts back up to the stained glass window. The
lines on the window emerge, a geometric formation floating in
mid air.*

                    AINSLEY (OVER)
               He's got his sights set on Wheeler Lab,
               that new military think tank at MIT.

*Nash's gaze carries the floating geometry across the crowd to
find the rainbows on the bar top. New lines rise, join the
pattern.*

                                                      (CONTINUED)

CONTINUED:

                    BENDER (OVER)
          They're only taking one this year. Best
          brain in the class.

                    AINSLEY (OVER)
          Hansen's used to being picked first.

*The new complex pattern rises, rotates slightly and is sucked
into the fractured pattern on Ainsley's tie. A perfect match.*

                    NASH
               (smiling)
          You know, there's a mathematical
          explanation for how horrible your tie is.

                    AINSLEY
          Nice. I'm Ainsley. Symbol Cryptography.

                    BENDER
          Ains here broke a Jap code. Helped rid the
          world of Fascism. Least that's what he
          tells the girls. The name's Bender. Atomic
          physics. And you are...

Just then a third FELLOW runs up, breathless. RICHARD SOL.

                    SOL
          Am I late?

Ainsley and Bender exchange a look. He's always late.

                    AINSLEY & BENDER
               Yes.

                    SOL
               (to Nash)
          Hi. I'm Sol.

Hansen separates from the crowd to join his friends.

                    HANSEN
          Ah the burden of genius. So many
          supplicants, so little time.

Hansen's eyes light on Nash. The beat of recognition is so
slight it's almost imperceptible. He smiles, raises his glass.

                    HANSEN (CONT'D)
          I'll take another.

                    NASH
          Excuse me.

(CONTINUED)

CONTINUED:

              HANSEN
    A thousand pardons. I simply assumed you
    were the waiter.

              SOL
    Play nice, Hansen.

              AINSLEY
    Nice is not Hansen's strong suit.

              HANSEN
    An honest mistake. What with those war
    ration shoes...

Nash's outfit, though stylishly formal, does look a bit dusty
compared to Hansen's elegant bohemia.

              HANSEN (CONT'D)
    That couture...

Hansen reaches forward, adjusts Nash's lapel. Not friendly. A
long beat. Then Nash smiles.

              NASH
    Well Martin, it is Martin, isn't it?

              HANSEN
    Why yes, John.

              NASH
    I imagine that by now you are indeed used
    to miscalculation. You see, I have read
    your pre-prints on both Nazi ciphers and
    non-linear equations and I am supremely
    confident that there is not a seminal or
    innovative idea in either one of them. I
    do hope to see you around.

With that, Nash offers a slight nod, walks off.

              SOL
    Who was that masked man?

              HANSEN
    Gentlemen meet John Nash. The mysterious
    West Virginia genius. The other winner of
    the distinguished Carnegie scholarship.

OFF Nash as he goes, stress like a mask on his face.

              VOICE (OVER)
    Mathematicians won the war...

INT.-PRINCETON-FACULTY LOUNGE-AFTERNOON

Immense. Oak panels. A silver haired professor, JOHN HELINGER,
stands on a podium, delivering the matriculation speech.

> HELINGER
> Mathematicians broke the Japanese codes and
> built the A-bomb...

PULL BACK OVER the crowd of students peering up at him.

> HELINGER (CONT'D)
> Mathematicians like you. But the flame of
> peace burns all too briefly. The Russians
> stated goal is global communism. In
> medicine or economics, technology or space,
> battle lines are being drawn. We stand on
> the edge of reason, gentlemen. On the
> frontier of human pursuit. To triumph we
> need results. Publishable. Applicable.
> Results.

HANSEN-CLOSE. Where he stands in the crowd.

> HELINGER (OVER) (CONT'D)
> Who among you will be the next Morse? The
> next Einstein?

NASH-CLOSE. Where he stands across the room.

> HELINGER (OVER) (CONT'D)
> Who among you will be the vanguard of
> democracy and freedom?

Helinger stares out at the sea of faces, his eyes burning.

> HELINGER (CONT'D)
> Today we bequeath America's future into
> your able hands. Welcome to Princeton.

EXT.-PRINCETON-BLAIR STEPS-SUNSET-SERIES OF SHOTS

(OVER) A MOTET plays. Nash descends steps to the commons. His
shadow seems to lag behind, out of step. Tall buildings loom.

EXT.-PRINCETON CAMPUS-SUNSET-SERIES OF SHOTS

Nash walks campus paths, head down, past students tossing
footballs, smoking against trees. His expression tight, anxious.

EXT.-PRINCETON-DORM-SUNSET

The sun is low in the sky. Nash walks into the tall dormitory.
(OVER) The MOTET VOICES continue, longing.

INT.-DORM ROOM-SUNSET

Nash is dragging his desk across the room. Positions it by the
window. He stares out at the sun-drenched field. Bravado gone.
Alone.

The door swings open behind him. Unruly hair and a tuxedo that
looks slept in whirl into the room. Meet CHARLES HERMAN, bags in
hand.

                    CHARLES
          The prodigal roommate arrives.

Charles turns down the MOTET, begins stripping as he speaks.
Nash stares in confusion as off come his jacket and bow-tie.

                    NASH
          Roommate?

                    CHARLES
          Did you know that a hangover is not having
          enough water in your body to run your Krebs
          cycle?

Charles pulls off his pants, and hopping, both shoes.

                    CHARLES (CONT'D)
          Which is exactly what happens when you die
          of thirst.

Now finally his shirt, which he throws on the couch.

                    CHARLES (CONT'D)
          So dying of thirst would feel like the
          hangover that finally kills you.

He grabs a towel and heads for the door.

                    CHARLES (CONT'D)
          Nash, right? Happy to meet you.

NASH-CLOSE. Speechless.

                                        CUT TO:

INT.-NASH'S DORM ROOM-SUNSET

A TOUCH FOOTBALL GAME-CLOSE. A HAND moves into FRAME, obscuring the players with wax symbols. The game begins. WIDER...

Nash has moved his desk in front of the windows, sits now, covering the players positions with symbols on the pane.

> CHARLES
> Officially almost human again.

Charles has ENTERED from the hall, hair wet, towel around his neck.

> CHARLES (CONT'D)
> Officer, I saw the driver who hit me. His name was Johnny Walker.

Nash continues to bear down on his work.

> CHARLES (CONT'D)
> I arrived last night. Right in time for English Department cocktails. The cock was mine. The tail belonged to a lovely young thing with a passion for D.H. Lawrence.

Nash nods, still doesn't look up from his work.

> CHARLES (CONT'D)
> You're not easily distracted, are you?

> NASH
> I am here to work.

> CHARLES
> I see.

Charles spots a bowl of cookies on Nash's desk. Nash covers the bowl before Charles can grab one, never once looking up.

That's when Charles actually climbs up on Nash's desk, sitting right in front of him.

> CHARLES (CONT'D)
> Is my roommate a dick?

Charles reaches into his pocket and pulls out something. A silver flask. Waves it in Nash's face.

> CHARLES (CONT'D)
> If we can't break the ice, how about we drown it?

EXT.-DORM ROOFTOP-SUNSET

Charles and Nash stand under the crimson sky, passing the flask.

              CHARLES
    So, how's it go? You the poor kid who
    didn't go to Exeter or Andover?

              NASH
    Despite my privileged upbringing, I am
    actually quite balanced. I have a chip on
    both shoulders.

              CHARLES
    Maybe you're just better with the old
    integers than with people?

              NASH
    My first-grade teacher once said I got
    two helpings of brain and half a helping
    of heart.

              CHARLES
    Note: send teacher a little Freud. Needs
    to brush up.

Nash LAUGHS. Takes a long swig.

              NASH
    The fact is, I don't like people much.
    And they don't much like me.

              CHARLES
    What, with all your wit and charm?

Nash smiles, looks out at the sun stained campus.

              CHARLES (CONT'D)
    Maths won't lead us to a higher truth,
    John... They're just boring.

Nash stares at him a beat. Then he smiles.

              NASH
    Do you know there are equations that can
    predict the rotation of galaxies as
    surely as the ebb and flow of human
    blood. There is a crystalline
    architecture to the universe we can only
    glimpse. That is the only truth. The math
    of things, the math of everything, the
    secrets implied by the world in whispers.

(CONTINUED)

CONTINUED:

                    CHARLES
          We are going to need more booze.

A couple of fellows race past, LAUGHING, tossing a football.

                    NASH
          Half of these school boys are already
          published. I cannot waste time with these
          classes, these books, memorizing the
          weaker assumptions of lesser mortals. I
          need to look through, to the governing
          dynamics, find a truly original idea. It
          is the only way I will distinguish
          myself. It is the only way I will...

                    CHARLES
          Matter.

Nash glances over to Charles, startled.

                    NASH
          Yes.

                    PROFESSOR (OVER)
          We study games to study human behavior in
          strategic conflict...

EXT.-FINE HALL-FALL-DAY-ESTABLISHING

The first hints of fall. Sol hurries into the building, late.

                    PROFESSOR (OVER)
          Put simply, the study of games is the
          study of war...

INT.-FINE HALL-CLASSROOM-DAY

PROFESSOR HORNER stands lecturing Bender, Hansen, Ainsley,
and several others. Sol pushes inside, late.

                    HORNER
          Thank you for stopping by Mr. Sol.

He glances at one empty chair. Then at his roster.

                    HORNER (CONT'D)
          Where the hell is...Nash?

Hansen looks out the window. FOLLOW Hansen's gaze into...

EXT.-PRINCETON-EAST PINE QUAD-DAY-CONTINUOUS

> HANSEN (OVER)
> He's looking for his original idea.

Nash is on his bicycle riding around the courtyard in figure eights, eyes half-closed, students scattering as he goes.

EXT.-PRINCETON-CANNON GREEN-DAY

Students sit over game boards set on benches. FIND one small group of familiar players.

> HANSEN (OVER)
> Cowards, all of you. Will none rise to meet
> my challenge?

Hansen stands over a GO board facing Bender, Ainsley and several others. RAPS the board with his knuckles.

> HANSEN (CONT'D)
> Come on, Bender, whoever wins, Sol does his
> laundry all semester...

> SOL
> Does this seem unfair to anyone else?

Others just shake their heads, GRUNT no's. Nash walks backwards past them.

> AINSLEY
> Hey Nash, taking a reverse
> constitutional?

Nash looks up, apparently startled by their presence.

> NASH (OVER)
> I hope to extract an algorithm to define
> their movements...

All follow Nash's gaze. A group of pigeons dance back and forth, devouring a pile of breadcrumbs.

> BENDER
> (mouthing)
> Psy-cho.

> SOL
> Man, I thought you dropped out. You ever
> gonna go to class?

CONTINUED:

                    NASH
       Classes dull the mind and destroy authentic
       creativity.

                   HANSEN
       John's going to stun us all with his
       genius.

Hansen flips a GO stone in the air, catches it in a fist.

                HANSEN (CONT'D)
       Which is another way of saying he doesn't
       have the nerve to compete.

Hansen RAPS the game table with his knuckles.

                HANSEN (CONT'D)
       Scared?

A beat. Then Nash smiles. Looks at Sol.

                   NASH
       No starch. Pressed and folded.

EXT.-PRINCETON-CANNON GREEN-DAY-MINUTES LATER

Nash faces Hansen across the GO board. The play is incredibly
fast. Nash is intense, almost preternaturally aware.

                   HANSEN
       Let me ask you something, John.

                   NASH
       Be my guest, Martin.

                   HANSEN
       Bender and Sol correctly completed Allen's
       proof of Peyrot's conjecture.

                   NASH
       Adequate work without innovation.

                    SOL
       I'm flattered. Are you flattered?

                 BENDER
       Flattered.

                 HANSEN
       I've got two weapons briefs under security
       review by the DOD.

CONTINUED:

> NASH
> Derivative drivel.

> HANSEN
> But Nash achievements: zero.

> NASH
> I'm a patient man, Martin. Is there an actual question coming?

> HANSEN
> What if you never come up with your original idea? How will it feel when I'm chosen for Wheeler and you're not?

Hansen makes a deft move, and strips Nash's stones.

> HANSEN (CONT'D)
> What if you lose?

Nash sits there. Stunned.

> NASH
> You should not have won. I had the first move. My play was perfect. The game is flawed.

> HANSEN
> Ah, the hubris of the defeated.

> NASH
> The game is flawed...

Nash stands, frustrated, inadvertently spilling the board. He walks off flustered. Hansen smiles, shakes his head.

> HANSEN
> Gentlemen, the great John Nash.

DISSOLVE TO:

EXT.-PRINCETON EAST PINE QUAD-SUNSET

Nash stares down at a GO board laying at his feet, his face lined with deep frustration.

*NASH-POV. Different sections of the board go dark, patterns of squares rising and falling, with ever increasing speed.*

PULL BACK AND UP...

EXT.-PRINCETON-CANNON GREEN-ACCELERATED TIME

HIGH ANGLE of Nash standing alone in the courtyard, head bowed.
The sun sinks behind the horizon; the moon moves across the
starry sky.

*NASH-POV. From the game board, a shape now rises, hexagonal,
hovering over the original play surface like a phantom.*

INT.-PRINCETON-STUDENT LOUNGE-DAY

Overstuffed chairs and scrawled notices on the walls. Sol and
another student passionately ARGUE a math problem on the
blackboard.

Nash ENTERS, walks up to Ainsley and Bender, who are playing GO,
and drops a hand-made hexagonal game board on top of their game.

                    BENDER
          What the hell-.

                    NASH
          Revised conflict parameters nullify variant
          outcome potential. Ideal move sequence
          guarantees first-player victory.
               (leaning in)
          If you win. You deserve to.

Nash holds Ainsley's gaze a beat too long. Then walks out.

                    BENDER
          He's totally lost it.

                    SOL
               (walking up)
          Somebody needs to cut down on their
          caffeine intake.

But Ainsley's not listening, he's staring at the new game board.

                    AINSLEY
          Will you look at this...

INT.-STUDENT LOUNGE-CONTINUOUS

Helinger enters with Hansen. Students sit over hexagonal game
boards.

                    HELINGER
          Your work on fusion is impressive.

                                        (CONTINUED)

CONTINUED:

                    HANSEN
          I know the boys at Wheeler are doing H-
          bomb research, sir. I'm hopeful-

Helinger has noticed Ainsley and another student playing on
the hexagonal board.

                    HELINGER
          What have we here, Mr. Ainsley?

                    AINSLEY
          This game. It's...perfect, sir.

                    HELINGER
          Where did it come from?

                    AINSLEY
               (wry smile)
          Well, it's called Nash, sir.

OFF Hansen's reaction. Less than pleased.

INT.-PRINCETON LIBRARY-LATE NIGHT

PUSH PAST the Librarian, PAST oak tables and green reading
lamps, FIND Nash drawing on a large window overlooking campus.

                    CHARLES (OVER)
          You've been here two days.

Nash turns to find Charles behind him. John looks exhausted.

                    NASH
          Hansen just published another paper. And I
          can't even find a topic for my doctorate.

Charles walks to the glass, appraises Nash's work.

                    CHARLES
          Hell, no. You invented window art.

                    NASH
               (off the first pattern)
          This group represents a game of touch
          football...
               (off the second pattern)
          This was a cluster of pigeons fighting for
          bread crumbs....
               (off the third)
          And this is a woman chasing a man who stole
          her purse....

                                              (CONTINUED)

CONTINUED:

                    CHARLES
          You watched a mugging?

                    NASH
          In competitive behavior, someone always
          loses...

                    CHARLES
          My niece knows that, John.
               (holds hand knee height)
          She's this tall.

                    NASH
          If I could derive an equilibrium where
          prevalence is a non-singular event, where
          nobody loses, imagine the effect on
          conflict scenarios, arms negotiations,
          currency exchange...

                    CHARLES
          When was the last time you ate?

Nash stares at him blankly.

                    CHARLES (CONT'D)
          You know, food?

                    NASH
          You have no respect for cognitive revery,
          do you know that?

                    CHARLES
          Pizza. I have respect for pizza. And
          beer...

Nash stares at his friend. Then drops his clipboard, follows.

                    NASH
          I have respect for beer.

EXT.-OLD HOME BAR-PRINCETON-NIGHT

Warm amber light shines through the window of the bar as
students push inside, out of the deepening cold.

INT.-OLD HOME BAR-NIGHT

(OVER) LES BROWN on the jukebox. Students party with coeds from
neighboring schools. Ainsley charms a few girls at the bar.

Nash is shooting pool. Alone. Hansen and Bender walk up.

                                                  (CONTINUED)

CONTINUED:

                 HANSEN
         Who's winning, you or you?

That's when Sol arrives. Late.

                 SOL
         Hey. Oh, hey, Nash. Where's Ains?

Bender gestures to the bar where Ainsley charms a few girls.

              SOL (CONT'D)
         I wish girls liked me like that.

                BENDER
         You wish girls liked you at all.

                HANSEN
         Hey, Nash, somebody's trying to get your
         attention.

Ainsley, arm now securely around a luscious brunette, is
gesturing Nash over. The blond GIGGLES, averts her eyes.

                BENDER
         Go with God.

                 SOL
         Come back a man.

                BENDER
         Fortune favors the brave.

                HANSEN
         Bombs away.

                NASH
         Before you scoff, gentlemen. May I remind
         you, the odds improve with each attempt.

Nash turns and heads towards the bar. Hansen stares after
him.

                HANSEN
         This will be classic.

INT.-OLD HOME BAR-MOMENTS LATER

Nash is at the bar with REBECCA, the blond coed. The two stand
in awkward silence. The moment stretches on. Finally...

                BECKY
         Maybe you want to buy me a drink.

                           (CONTINUED)

CONTINUED:


Nash appraises her clinically.

                    NASH
          Look, I don't know exactly what things I
          am required to say in order for you to
          have intercourse with me. But could we
          assume I have said them? I mean
          essentially we're talking about fluid
          exchange, right? So, could we go right to
          the sex?

                    BECKY
          That was sweet.

She SLAPS him across the face.

                    BECKY (CONT'D)
          Have a nice night, asshole.

She walks off. John turns to face the bar.

                    VOICE (OVER)
          Want a piece of friendly advice?

WIDER. Charles is standing at the juke-box behind him.

                    NASH
          Is 'no' an actual option?

                    CHARLES
          You may be a genius, but when it comes to
          the calculus of human emotions, you don't
          have a clue. So buy them drinks. Smile. Nod
          a lot. And keep your bloody mouth shut.

Charles CLAPS him on the shoulder.

                    CHARLES (CONT'D)
          I especially like the fluid exchange
          part.

Charles heads out the door, slipping past an ENTERING JOCK.

                    NASH
          What's unfriendly advice sound like?

Nash turns to face the Jock who stares back, face puzzled.

EXT.-PRINCETON-HOLDER ARCHES-WINTER-DAY-WIDE ANGLE

Two figures pass through the icy stone archways.


                                        (CONTINUED)

CONTINUED:

                    HELINGER (OVER)
      Perhaps your academic progress has suffered
      from too much isolation...

EXT.-PRINCETON-HOLDER ARCHWAYS-WALKING

Nash and Helinger walk through patterns of winter sun.

                    HELINGER
      Human connection gives us perspective.
      Friends...

                    NASH
      I don't make friends.

                    HELINGER
      Why not?

                    NASH
      Apparently I'm an asshole.

                    HELINGER
      The faculty is completing mid year reviews.
      We're deciding which placement applications
      to support.

                    NASH
      Wheeler would be my first choice, sir.

Helinger stares at him incredulously.

                    HELINGER
      John, your fellows have attended classes,
      written papers, published-.

                    NASH
      I am still searching for-.

                    HELINGER
      Your original idea, I know. But there are
      eight weeks until the end of the semester
      and essentially all you've done is create
      a game. Clever, John. But just nowhere
      near good enough.

Helinger opens a door, Nash trailing him into...

INT.-PRINCETON-MATH LOUNGE-DAY-CONTINUOUS

A cloak chamber leads to a room where math faculty are served
tea by tuxedoed waiters. A valet stands at the archway.

                                      (CONTINUED)

CONTINUED:

>                    NASH
>           I've been working on manifold embedding,
>           also my bargaining stratagems have been
>           showing some promise, and if you would
>           just be kind enough to get me another
>           meeting with Professor Einstein, as I
>           have repeatedly asked you for, I am
>           confident that this time he would be more
>           impressed with my revisions on his theory
>           of general relativity.

Helinger has handed his coat to the valet.

>                    HELINGER
>           Do you see what they are doing, John?

Beyond, a professor rises, crosses the room. Takes his pen
from his pocket, lays it in front of a seated man.

>                    HELINGER (CONT'D)
>           The pens is one of the oldest tributes here
>           at Princeton.

More and more faculty are rising, now, lying their pens down in
front of the smiling man.

>                    HELINGER (CONT'D)
>           Reserved for a member of the department who
>           makes the achievement of a lifetime.

Helinger takes his own pen from his pocket. Then he notices the
hunger in Nash's eyes.

>                    HELINGER (CONT'D)
>           What do you see?

>                    NASH
>           Recognition.

>                    HELINGER
>           Try seeing accomplishment.

>                    NASH
>           Is there a difference?

Helinger just shakes his head, stares at him sadly.

>                    HELINGER
>           You haven't focused. I am sorry but up to
>           this point your record doesn't warrant any
>           placement at all. Good day.

Helinger walks into the main room, leaving John looking in.

INT.-NASH'S DORM ROOM-LATE AFTERNOON-WINTER

Nash stands, forehead against the window, staring out. The glass
is covered with elaborate wax patterns.

>                    NASH
>          I can't see it. There's nothing there.

Nash raps his head on the window, cracking the glass.

>                    CHARLES (OVER)
>          Jesus.

WIDER. Charles is sitting up on the couch, looking sleepy, sheet
around his shoulders.

>                    CHARLES (CONT'D)
>          Let's get out of here, go make a bit of
>          trouble, hell, a lot of trouble-.

Nash looks up, rivulets of blood running down his forehead. When
his VOICE comes now there is a defeat that is chilling.

>                    NASH
>          I can't fail.

Charles rubs his wrist.

>                    CHARLES
>          Oh, I know this drill.

>                    NASH
>          This is all I am.

Nash grabs the end of the desk, starts to pull it away.

>                    NASH (CONT'D)
>          I can't keep staring into space. There's
>          nothing there. No secret whispers, no
>          crystal palace-.

Charles grabs his arm, spinning him back towards him.

>                    CHARLES
>          You want to do some damage, don't fool
>          around.

John pulls away from Charles, grabs the desk again, begins
dragging it away from the window.

>                    NASH
>          I will face the wall. I'll read their
>          books, attend their classes-

                                                    (CONTINUED)

CONTINUED:


Charles crosses as Nash continues dragging the desk.

>                    CHARLES
>          Come on now. You wanted to break your head
>          open, then do it.

And Charles shoves him, hard, in the chest.

>                    CHARLES (CONT'D)
>          Break it.
>               (shoves him harder)
>          Go on!
>               (harder still)
>          Bust that worthless egg wide open.

One final shove. And this time, Nash shoves back. Hard. Sending
Charles SLAMMING into the wall.

>                    NASH
>          Godammit, Charles, what the hell is your
>          problem-.

Nash stands over him. Furious. Ready to fight.

>                    CHARLES
>          Not my problem, my friend...

As Charles stands now, he is grinning.

>                    CHARLES (CONT'D)
>          Not your problem...

Charles grabs the end of the desk.

>                    CHARLES (CONT'D)
>          Their problem.

Charles begins shoving the desk towards the window. The desk
HITS and SMASHES through the glass.

EXT.-DORM ROOM-LATE AFTERNOON-WINTER

The desk blows through the window, tumbling two stories to the
snowy ground in an EXPLOSION of wood and floating paper.

Nash leans out, looking down at the twirling star of still
settling debris.

INT.-DORM ROOM-CONTINUOUS

Nash pulls his head inside, stares at Charles, blown out by sun.


(CONTINUED)

CONTINUED:

                    CHARLES
      Heavy.

Nash nods, can't help a shocked grin.

                    CHARLES (CONT'D)
      Isaac Newton was right.

                    NASH
      He was on to something.

And with that, both boys burst into LAUGHTER. Then Charles
looks at Nash.

                    CHARLES
      Your answer isn't, face the wall. It's not
      in their books and classes.

Charles gestures out the broken window.

                    CHARLES (CONT'D)
      It's out there, where you've been looking.
      When they tell you to look away, you've
      just got to look closer. Do you understand?

                    NASH
      You're kind of strange, aren't you?

                    CHARLES
      Coming from you, do you have any idea how
      much that scares me?

INT.-OLD HOME BAR-NIGHT-WINTER

(OVER) Sinatra on the juke. John sits at a table strewn with
books, drawing Escher-like patterns on endless cocktail napkins.
Hansen, Sol, Bender, and Ainsley play pool.

                    BENDER
      Nash looks a little down. I think he's
      still in mourning.

                    SOL
      That desk was so young, so full of
      promise.

                    AINSLEY
      Incoming.

Ainsley is gesturing to the door. About six women have entered.
Well, five and one. The BLOND in the lead is simply, perfect.

PAN ACROSS the guys' stunned faces.

                                (CONTINUED)

CONTINUED:

                    HANSEN
     With me.

FAVOR the boys as they follow Hansen to Nash's table, a better
vantage point from which to ogle the now sitting girls.

                    NASH
     I'm still not buying the beer-
         (follows their gaze)
     Oh.
         (off the blond)
     Does anyone else feel like she should be
     moving in slow motion?

                    HANSEN
     I'm going to get her a drink.

                    NASH
     That's highly original.

                    BENDER
     Will she want a large wedding?

                    AINSLEY
     One beauty, too many suitors.

                    SOL
     Swords, gentlemen? Pistols at dawn?

Already a few beers to the wind, Hansen TAPS the book John was
reading. Studies in Modern Economics.

                    HANSEN
     Have you learned nothing gentlemen?
     Remember the benevolent hand of your pater
     familias. Recall the lesson of Adam Smith,
     the father of modern economics.

                    SOL
         (by route)
     In competition, individual ambition serves
     the common good.

                    AINSLEY
     Every man for himself.

                    BENDER
     Those who strike out end up with her
     friends.

John nods. Then his gaze fixes on the girls.

                              (CONTINUED)

CONTINUED:

>           SOL
> She's looking over. I think she's looking
> at Nash.

>           HANSEN
> He may have the advantage now. But wait
> until he opens his mouth.

>           NASH
> Adam Smith was wrong.

>           HANSEN
> What are you talking about?

*NASH-POV. The girls' table grows dark, only the blond girl highlighted, moving into the foreground.*

>           NASH (OVER)
> If everyone competes for the blond...

*NASH-POV. Images of all the boys surround the blond, then blow apart like fragments of glass, leaving the blond standing alone.*

>           NASH (OVER) (CONT'D)
> ...We block each other and no one gets her.

*NASH-POV. The other girls rise into the foreground, images of our boys pairing off with them.*

>           NASH (OVER) (CONT'D)
> ...So then we go for her friends...

*NASH-POV. All the other girls suddenly go dark, leaving our group standing alone.*

>           NASH (OVER) (CONT'D)
> ...But they give us the cold shoulder,
> because no one likes to be second choice.
> Again, no winner.

*NASH-POV. The blond girl goes dark.*

>           NASH (OVER) (CONT'D)
> ...But what if none of us go for the
> blond...

*NASH-POV. Now images of the boys pair up with the remaining girls.*

>           NASH (CONT'D)
> ...We don't get in each other's way, we
> don't insult the other girls.

(CONTINUED)

CONTINUED:


*NASH-POV. The world goes dark except for the couples who twirl like a mobile of arabesques in a victorious swirl.*

>           NASH (OVER) (CONT'D)
> That's the only way we win. That's the only
> way we all get laid.

All are staring at him.

>           NASH (CONT'D)
> Adam Smith said the best outcome for the
> group comes from everyone trying to do
> what's best for himself. Incorrect. The
> best outcome results from everyone trying
> to do what's best for himself <u>and</u> the
> group.

>           HANSEN
> Nash, if this is some plan for you to get
> the blond alone...

>           NASH
> Governing dynamics gentlemen. Adam Smith
> was wrong.

And with that, Nash rises and heads off across the bar. Hansen stares after him, face darkening with concern.

>           SOL
> Could he be weirder?

The Blond looks up at Nash as he approaches, hopeful, but he just blows by her, heading for the door. The guys sit, silent.

>           SOL (CONT'D)
> What the hell?

>           BENDER
> I'm game.

They all rise and make for the girls.

>                                    CUT TO:

SYMBOLS being furiously wrought on a legal pad. PULL BACK...

INT.-NASH'S DORM ROOM-DAWN-WINTER

Nash sits over his desk working. The room looks like a tornado hit. Open books, cut up math journals. PULL OUT...

EXT.-NASH'S DORM-ACCELERATED TIME

Within the window, time passes normally, Nash continuing to
work. Outside, snow covers the building, then melts and tendrils
of ivy snake up the concrete facade and bloom, all while Nash
works on.

INT.-HELINGER'S OFFICE-DAY-SPRING-1949

Helinger sits across the desk from Nash, holding Nash's
handwritten paper in his hand.

> HELINGER
> And you came up with this on a dating
> excursion?

> NASH
> Well, it was either mathematics or
> another bag of pretzels.

> HELINGER
> You do realize this flies in the face of
> one hundred and fifty years of economic
> theory?

> NASH
> That I do, sir.

> HELINGER
> And that it is rather presumptuous, don't
> you think?

> NASH
> Yes, it is sir.

Helinger stares at the young man.

> HELINGER
> Well, Mr. Nash, I have to admit the work is
> good.

> NASH
> Good?

> HELINGER
> All right, more than good. It may be the
> single most important work on competitive
> bargaining I have ever seen.

Helinger drops the paper on his desk.

(CONTINUED)

CONTINUED:

> HELINGER (CONT'D)
> Well, it appears you'll get any placement
> you like, Mr. Nash.

Nash glances up. Charles stands in the hallway through the slightly open door. Nash gives a small nod. Charles grins.

> HELINGER (CONT'D)
> Most of the top programs will ask you to
> recommend two team members. Stills and
> Frank are excellent choices-.

> NASH
> ...I'll take Sol and Bender, sir.

> HELINGER
> Sol and Bender-. Sol and Bender are
> extraordinary mathematicians. Has it
> occurred to you, Mr. Nash, that Sol and
> Bender might have plans of their own?

Nash just smiles.

INT.-OLD HOME BAR-SPRING-DAY

Sol and Bender, arms around two coeds from the bar, POP champagne bottles as STUDENTS congratulate them.

> BENDER
> Okay, awkward moment...

Another figure steps from the crowd. Nash walks right up to Hansen, stands facing him now, too close. Holds his eyes.

Then Nash reaches forward and simply fingers Hansen's lapel, an echo of Hansen's taunt at the reception. A beat. Endless.

Finally, Hansen offers the slightest of bows and, then, a wry, grudging smile. More WHOOPS as CELEBRATION resumes.

Nash notices a broken ashtray on the bar. He lifts a coaster, turns it, once, twice, then drops it over the ashtray, making a five-pointed shape...

> DISSOLVE TO:

EXT.-THE PENTAGON-WASHINGTON DC-DAY-1953

Sun breaks on the monolithic stone building.

> CAPTAIN (OVER)
> General, the analyst from Wheeler Lab is
> here.

INT.-THE PENTAGON-WAR ROOM-DAY

Lit map-boards of the cold war globe. The hulking behemoths of
early IBM computers. A GENERAL stands with two TECHNICIANS and a
senior ANALYST before a wall, papered with sheets of numbers.

                    GENERAL
          Show him in.

A CAPTAIN hits a button. A red wall light goes green. A MAN in a
raincoat ENTERS, face obscured by the shadow of his hat.

                    CAPTAIN
          General, this is Wheeler team leader...

The Man removes his hat to reveal...

                    CAPTAIN (CONT'D)
          ...Dr. John Nash.

Razor cool, perfectly comfortable in his own skin. Four years
since we have seen him.

                    GENERAL
          Glad you could come, Doctor.

Nash nods. Hands his overcoat to a technician. He is wearing a
slim black suit and tie. The General nods to the Analyst.

                    ANALYST
          We have been intercepting radio
          transmissions from Moscow.

                    GENERAL
          The computer can't detect a pattern. But
          I'm sure it's code.

                    NASH
          Why is that, General?

                    GENERAL
          Ever just know something, Dr. Nash?

Nash smiles.

                    NASH
          Constantly.

Nash moves to the wall papered with code.

                    GENERAL
          We have developed several ciphers...

                                        (CONTINUED)

CONTINUED:


But Nash just walks away from the officer. He stands facing the
wall, staring at the numbers.

PUSH IN ON Nash's eyes. In the black ocean of his pupils, the
reflected rows of code begin to move, forming shifting patterns.

PULL BACK ON Nash, still staring at the wall. Hours have passed,
folks sitting, jackets hanging on chair backs, coffee cups
empty.

*NASH-POV. Series of numbers darken as others rise, a cascade of
rapidly changing patterns, endless permutations until...*

                    NASH
          There.

Nash pulls a pencil from his pocket, begins writing numbers on
his clipboard. All stare.

                    NASH (CONT'D)
          I need a map. North America I think.

The General and the Analyst exchange a look. The General nods
and the Captain illuminates a map Board of North America.

                    NASH (CONT'D)
          Starkey Corners, Maine. 48, 03, 01, North.
          91, 26, 35, West. Prairie Portage,
          Minnesota. These are longitudes and
          latitudes.

Nash is already marking the map board.

                    NASH (CONT'D)
          There are at least ten others. They appear
          to be routing orders. Ways across the
          border into the US.

Nash glances upwards. From a glass booth overlooking the room, a
MAN is watching him. Fine dark suit. Thin tie. WILLIAM PARCHER.

                    NASH (CONT'D)
          Who's Big Brother?

                    GENERAL
          Excuse me?

But when Nash looks up again, the booth is empty. The man has
gone.

                    NASH
          What are the Russians moving, General?


                                             (CONTINUED)

CONTINUED:


But the General just claps his shoulder, already turning away.

> GENERAL
> (dismissive)
> You've done your country a great service,
> son.

The men begin tearing down the sheets of code from the wall.

EXT.-MIT CAMPUS-CAMBRIDGE-AFTERNOON-SUMMER

A black sedan is waved through a checkpoint by two uniformed
soldiers. The car passes through the gate into...

EXT.-MIT-WHEELER LAB COMPOUND-AFTERNOON

High fences. A section of buildings that essentially comprise a
small military base in the center of MIT's campus.

Nash emerges from the car, past scholars and military personnel.
Vanishes into a large, single story building. Wheeler
headquarters.

INT.-MIT-WHEELER HEADQUARTERS-WALKING

Bustling. And hot. Nash is walking down a long, sun-lit
corridor. A fellow falls into step with him. It's Sol.

> SOL
> Home run at the Pentagon.

> NASH
> Have they actually taken the word
> classified out of the dictionary?

> SOL
> Please. This is the military. The only
> place information travels faster is high
> school.

> NASH
> Sol, how about you call me chief or boss or
> something?

> SOL
> How about you blow yourself?

> NASH
> That's what I figured.

Nash strips off his jacket. Another figure falls into step with
them, a file folder in his hand. Bender.

(CONTINUED)

CONTINUED:

                    BENDER
          Air conditioning broke again.

                    NASH
          Exactly how am I supposed to save the world
          if I am melting in here?

INT.-MIT-WHEELER HEADQUARTERS-NASH'S OFFICE-CONTINUOUS

Large. Sunlit. Walls covered with mathematical symbols,
technical schematics. Nash peels off his shirt, leaving only
his T.

                    NASH
          Only two trips to The Pentagon in four
          years.

                    SOL
          That's two more than we've had.

                    BENDER
               (hands Nash a file)
          It gets better. I've reviewed our
          scintillating new assignment.

                    NASH
          Moscow has the H-bomb. The Nazis are
          repatriating South America. China has a
          standing army of 2.8 million...
               (slaps the file on the desk)
          And we're doing stress tests for a new dam.

Nash begins rifling his mail. A letter to Charles Herman at
Cambridge University. Stamped: Return To Sender-Address Unknown.

                    BENDER
          You made the cover of Fortune. Again.

                    SOL
          Please note the use of you not we.

FORTUNE-CLOSE. Nash lifts the magazine from his mail pile. The
cover reads, America's Geniuses. Four portraits. John looks
pissed.

                    NASH
          It was supposed to be just me. First, they
          rob me of the Fields Medal and now I have
          to share the cover with these hacks, these
          scholars of trivia.

                                        (CONTINUED)

CONTINUED:

                    BENDER
          John, exactly what's the difference between
          genius and most genius?

                    NASH
          Quite a lot, actually.

                    SOL
               (rolling his eyes)
          He's your son.

Bender pulls something from the mail pile. Tears off the
paper wrapper. It's a brand new textbook.

                    BENDER
          Anyway, you've got ten minutes-

                    NASH
          I've always got ten minutes.

                    SOL
          Before your new class.

NASH-CLOSE. Actually pales.

                    NASH
          Can't I get a note from a doctor?

                    BENDER
          You are a Doctor. And no. You know the
          drill. We get facilities...

                    SOL
          MIT gets America's great minds of today
          teaching America's great minds of tomorrow.
          Poor bastards.

Sol thrusts the textbook into Nash's arms.

                    BENDER
          Have a nice day at school.

                    SOL
          Bell's ringing.

                    NASH
               (heading for the door)
          Screw you both. Really.

And with that, he's gone.

CONTINUED:


                          BENDER
              Oh to be a fly on the wall.


                                                  CUT TO:


A HARD HAT is JACK-HAMMERING one of the cement walkways.
DEAFENING. PULL BACK THROUGH A WINDOW TO REVEAL...

INT.-MIT CLASSROOM-AFTERNOON

(OVER) The CONSTRUCTION RACKET. Maybe two dozen grad students
sit restlessly at their desks, sweating, fanning themselves,
windows open to the meager breeze.

Nash ENTERS in his T-shirt, tosses the textbook into the trash,
then stares out at the class like a soldier eyeing the enemy.

                          NASH
              What the hell is that racket?

Nash begins closing windows, shutting out the CONSTRUCTION
NOISE.

                          STUDENT
              Can we leave one open Professor? It's
              really hot, sir...

Nash has returned to the board. Turns to face the boy who spoke.

                          NASH
              Your comfort comes second to my ability to
              hear my own voice. Personally, I am certain
              this class will be a deadly waste of both
              your, and worse, my time. But, here we are.
              Attend or not. Complete the assignments at
              your whim. We begin.

PAN across the stunned faces. A beat. Nash returns to the board.

                          NASH (CONT'D)
              This problem should take you several months
              to solve....

Nash trails off. A YOUNG WOMAN has risen. Exquisite. Powerfully
intelligent eyes. Moving like water. This is ALICIA LARDE.

                          NASH (CONT'D)
              Miss...

She crosses the room, turns now and holds Nash's gaze a beat.
Then she pushes open a window.


                                              (CONTINUED)

CONTINUED:


Folks just stare, stunned, as she pokes her head outside, begins
TALKING. We hear only random WORDS, then LAUGHTER.

THROUGH THE WINDOW. The Construction Workers move off.

See the look she gives him, as stunning as it is impassable. A
beat. Then Nash offers the barest nod. Turns back to the board.

                    NASH (CONT'D)
               As I was saying, this problem will take
               some of you a few months to solve, some of
               you the rest of your lives...

PULL BACK over Nash as Alicia continues around the room, opening
every window to the breeze.

EXT.-MIT-WHEELER HEADQUARTERS-NIGHT

Nash is descending the front steps towards the main doors.

                    VOICE (OVER)
               Professor Nash...

Standing at the foot of the steps is a single figure. Slim black
suit. Thin tie. It takes Nash a beat to recognize him as the man
from the Pentagon.

                    PARCHER
               William Parcher.
                    (holds out an ID)
               Big Brother at your service.

Nash inspects the Department of Defense photo and badge,
embossed with government seal. Looks up into the most uncanny
eyes.

                    NASH
               So, what can I do for the Department of
               Defense.
                    (wry)
               You going to give me a raise?

EXT.-MIT-WHEELER LAB COMPOUND-NIGHT-WALKING

Parcher is leading Nash away past the main building, deeper into
the fenced off military compound.

                    PARCHER
               Impressive work at the Pentagon.

                    NASH
               Yes. It was.


                                        (CONTINUED)

CONTINUED:

                    PARCHER
          Oppenheimer used to say genius sees the
          answer before the question.

                    NASH
          You knew Oppenheimer?

                    PARCHER
          His project was under my supervision.

                    NASH
          Which project?
               (eyes widening)
          That project?

Nash stops, impressed. Parcher just shakes his head.

                    PARCHER
          It's not that simple, you know.

                    NASH
          You ended the war.

                    PARCHER
          We incinerated two hundred thousand people
          in a heartbeat.

                    NASH
          Great deeds come at great cost, Mr.
          Parcher.

Parcher's smile, coming now, is very old.

                    PARCHER
          Conviction, it turns out, is a luxury of
          those on the sidelines.

William and John approach a guard-post.

                    NASH
               (flashing his ID)
          This is a secure area...

But the guard just salutes and the two walk on, heading
deeper into the complex.

                    PARCHER
          They know me. So, no close friends. No
          family. Why is that, John?

                    NASH
          I like to think I'm a lone wolf. But mostly
          people just don't like me.

                                        (CONTINUED)

CONTINUED:


Parcher's LAUGH catches Nash by surprise.

                    PARCHER
          There are endeavors where your lack of
          personal connection would be considered an
          advantage.

                    NASH
          And what might those be?

                    PARCHER
          I know these last four years may have
          seemed...disappointing.

                    NASH
          Two stress fracture assessments, four
          power grid reviews, and that riveting
          study on the effects of gum-chewing
          during combat.

                    PARCHER
          Has it occurred to you John that
          sometimes the research isn't what we're
          evaluating. Your life exists on the
          surface of a mighty ocean. What lies
          underneath, forces colliding, ready to
          break the surface at any moment and
          shatter the calm, that's my world.

                    NASH
          Good speech.

                    PARCHER
          It should be.
               (sad smile)
          I've made it enough times.

They have come to a row of warehouses at the rear of the
compound. All abandoned, paint chipping, windows boarded up.

                    PARCHER (CONT'D)
          Ever been here?

                    NASH
          We were told during our initial briefing
          these warehouses were abandoned.

They have arrived at a warehouse at the end of the row. A
uniformed soldier stands guard. He salutes.

                    PARCHER
          That's not precisely accurate.

                                        (CONTINUED)

CONTINUED:


The soldier pulls the door open.

INT.-MIT-WHEELER COMPOUND-PARCHER'S WAREHOUSE

Sprawling. White suited technicians scurry back and forth amidst
hi-tech computing machines.

>           NASH
>      Half this technology is a good ten years
>      off.

Parcher leads Nash through the maze of equipment towards a large
glass office.

INT.-PARCHER'S OFFICE

Nash sits across the desk. Photos of Parcher with Roosevelt;
with Einstein; in a Colonel's uniform with an allied liberation
force at the gates of a concentration camp.

>           PARCHER
>         (noticing his gaze)
>      Dachau. Man is capable of as much atrocity
>      as he has imagination.

Parcher looks off a beat. Eyes that have seen too much. Then...

>           PARCHER (CONT'D)
>      By telling you what I am about to tell you
>      I am increasing your security clearance to
>      Top Secret.

Parcher slides a form with a government watermark across the
desk.

>           PARCHER (CONT'D)
>      Whether or not you agree to assist in this
>      operation, disclosure of secure information
>      can result in imprisonment. Get it?

>           NASH
>      What operation?

>           PARCHER
>      Please sign.

John signs the form, slides it back. William nods. Then he lifts
a small remote control, points it at a blank TV screen in the
wall.

>           NASH
>         (off the remote)
>      Those are a good idea.

                                              (CONTINUED)

CONTINUED:


ON SCREEN-A placard reading Eyes Only is replaced by black and whites of a giant factory, US soldiers scattered in every frame.

                    PARCHER (OVER)
          This factory is in Berlin. We seized it at
          the end of the war.

ON SCREEN-Closer shots of large, complex production equipment.

                    PARCHER (CONT'D)
          Nazi engineers were attempting to build a
          portable atomic bomb.

                    NASH
          That is simply not possible.

Parcher looks up at John a beat, then back to the screen which now shows a device no larger than a television.

                    PARCHER
          I'm afraid it is. The Soviets reached this
          facility before we did. We lost the damn
          thing.

Parcher just stares at him, letting this sink in.

                    NASH
          The routing orders at the Pentagon. They
          were for this, weren't they?

                    PARCHER
          The Soviets aren't as unified as people
          believe. A faction of the Red Army calling
          itself Novaya Svobga ---The New Freedom---
          has control of the bomb and intends to
          detonate it on U.S. soil. Their plan is to
          incur maximum civilian casualties.

                    NASH
          We've run the simulations. Any domestic
          strike scenario results in full-scale
          nuclear war. Why would the Russians want
          that?

                    PARCHER
          Because they can win.

Simple as that.

                    PARCHER (CONT'D)
          New Freedom has sleeper agents here in the
          U.S. McCarthy is an idiot. Unfortunately,
          that doesn't make him wrong.
                    (MORE)

CONTINUED:

                    PARCHER (CONT'D)
      New Freedom is communicating to its agents
      through codes embedded in periodicals and
      newspapers. That's where you come in.

                    NASH
      I'm listening.

                    PARCHER
      You see, John, what distinguishes you is
      that you are, quite simply, the best
      natural code breaker I have ever seen.

Nash stares at him.

                    NASH
      Tell me what you want me to do.

INT.-PARCHER'S WAREHOUSE-MOMENTS LATER

Nash and William stand over a monitor manned by a technician.

                    PARCHER
      Commit this list of periodicals to memory.

John looks at the list. Nods.

                    PARCHER (CONT'D)
      Scan each new issue. Find any hidden codes.
      Decipher them.

                                DISSOLVE TO:

INT.-PARCHER'S WAREHOUSE-MOMENTS LATER

Parcher stands with John at another work-station. A
technician has lowered what appears to be large x-ray machine
over his arm.

                    TECHNICIAN
      This may be uncomfortable.

The machine makes contact with John's arm and HISSES.

                    NASH
      What the-?

The technician lifts the machine, shines a black light over
John's wrist. In a fresh welt above his wrist we see a
series of numbers.

                    PARCHER
      We have implanted a radium diode under
      your skin. It's perfectly safe. These
      numbers will change over time.
                    (MORE)

                                  (CONTINUED)

CONTINUED:

                    PARCHER (CONT'D)
          They are access codes to your drop spot.
          Here is its location...

                                        DISSOLVE TO:


EXT.-PARCHER'S WAREHOUSE-SUNSET

John emerges from the door, blinking into the dying light.

                    PARCHER (OVER)
          You can tell no one of your work.  Just
          proceed with normal life.  Avoid new
          people.  And, assume at all times your
          are being watched.

                    NASH
          So what am I now?  A spy?

PULL BACK AND UP over John standing in the courtyard.  Alone.

INT.-MIT-WHEELER HEADQUARTERS-NASH'S OFFICE

A LIFE MAGAZINE-CLOSE. A PEN ENTERS FRAME circles certain
occurrences of certain words, then crosses them out. WIDER.

Nash sits behind his desk, pen in hand, the very picture of
focused efficiency. (OVER) a KNOCK.

                    NASH
          Come.

Nash looks up to see a figure standing in his doorway. Alicia, a
soldier-escort behind her.

                    ALICIA
          Boy, you must really be important.

Nash stares a beat. Then he shakes his head.

                    NASH
          It's all right, Mike.

The Soldier tips his hat to Alicia and is gone.

                    NASH (CONT'D)
          How did you get in here?

Alicia throws her hair and giggles, the very picture of a sex
kitten.  Then she brings the intelligence back into her eyes.

                    ALICIA
          Testosterone is a girl's best friend.

Alicia steps into the room.

                                        (CONTINUED)

CONTINUED:


                         ALICIA (CONT'D)
              What are you working on?

                         NASH
              Classified.

                         ALICIA
              Come on. Tell.

                         NASH
              Ask me again, I get to shoot you.

Alicia can't help but LAUGH.

                         ALICIA
              Everybody waited half an hour.

                         NASH
              For?

                         ALICIA
              Class. You missed class today.

                         NASH
              Ah well, I am confident they did not miss
              me.

He resumes working. Alicia slides a single page atop his
magazine.

                         ALICIA
              The problem you left on the board. I solved
              it.

Nash barely glances at her paper as he hands it back.

                         NASH
              No. You didn't.

                         ALICIA
              You didn't even look.

                         NASH
              I never said the vector fields were
              rational functions.

Alicia stares at him. Then looks back at her equation. Frowns.

                         NASH (CONT'D)
                    (without looking up)
              Your solution is elegant though ultimately
              incorrect.

(CONTINUED)

CONTINUED:


Alicia beams. Nash continues to work. She doesn't move.

                    NASH (CONT'D)
          You're still here.

                    ALICIA
          I'm still here.

                    NASH
          Why?

                    ALICIA
          I was wondering, Professor Nash, if I could
          ask you to dinner.

Nash looks up at her. Stunned.

                    ALICIA (CONT'D)
          You do eat, don't you?

                    NASH
          On occasion. Table for one. You know how it
          is. Promethius, chained to the rock, birds
          circling overhead.  No, I expect you
          wouldn't.

He sizes her up. A long beat, then...

                    NASH (CONT'D)
          Leave your address with my office. I'll
          pick you up Friday at eight. ...We'll eat.

Nash goes back to work. Alicia smiles, starts for the door. Nash
calls after...

                    NASH (CONT'D)
          One more thing.

Alicia turns back to him, sunlight through the window striking
her face so perfectly it steals your breath.

                    NASH (CONT'D)
          Do you have a name or should I just call
          you miss?

EXT.-BOSTON-GOVERNOR'S MANSION-NIGHT

Hundreds of tiny white lights illuminate the giant stone
mansion, glittering in the darkness like a Christmas ornament.
Limos pulling into the circular drive, disgorging passengers.

                    NASH (OVER)
          Governor, may I present...

INT.-GOVERNOR'S MANSION-NIGHT

A resplendent black tie party. Nash stands in the foyer, poised and dashing.

> ALICIA
> Miss Alicia Larde.

WIDER. Smiling beside Nash in a stunning black dress is Alicia. A PHOTOGRAPHER steps forward.

> PHOTOGRAPHER
> Professor, you and the Governor...

Nash and the Governor strike a posed handshake. But Alicia steps into the shot, begins adjusting Nash's bow-tie.

> ALICIA
> No, no. I'll want a copy of this, first big date and all, so you boys need to look good....

She brushes Nash's lapel, pulls a handkerchief from her purse and slips the folded cloth into his breast pocket.

> ALICIA (CONT'D)
> ...Which is not a state you find yourselves in altogether naturally.

Alicia moves John's hair, steps back, appraises her work.

> ALICIA (CONT'D)
> Better. Yummy, even.

The Governor notes John's mildly startled smile.

> ALICIA (CONT'D)
> I'm surprising him.

> GOVERNOR
> You just keep on surprising him.

> The FRAME WHITENS in a FLASH...

INT.-GOVERNOR'S MANSION-MOMENTS LATER

Alicia and Nash inspect a painting on the wall. Alicia is riveted.

> ALICIA
> God must be a painter. Why else would we have so many colors?

(CONTINUED)

CONTINUED:


Nash nods. He's looking over her shoulder at two dark-suited MEN on the balcony. They notice his gaze, look away.

                    NASH
                (distracted)
          So, you're a painter?

                    ALICIA
          That's not actually what I said.

She raises her hand. Faint paint-stains color her skin.

                    ALICIA (CONT'D)
          But, yes. I am.

The two Men on the balcony are clocking Nash again. When they catch his eyes, they move off.

                    ALICIA (CONT'D)
          I'm also a burlesque dancer...

Nash nods, still following the Men with his eyes.

                    ALICIA (CONT'D)
          I started stripping for infantry in France,
          then moved up to fly boys.

                    NASH
          Um-hmm.

He's still staring across the room. That's when she actually grabs his bow tie and pulls his head to face her.

                    ALICIA
          Here. Me. Your date.

Nash looks at her. Smiles.

                    NASH
          Practice human comportment and social
          interaction.

She nods, again all warmth.

                    ALICIA
          Now that's a plan. Champagne would be
          lovely. I'll be outside.

EXT.-GOVERNOR'S MANSION-LATER

Alicia stands on a terrace looking out at the city.  Nash arrives, hands her a beading flute of champagne.


(CONTINUED)

CONTINUED:

                    ALICIA
          Thank you.

Nash pulls her handkerchief from his pocket. Fine silk with a
small embroidered rose. Starts to hand it back.

                    ALICIA (CONT'D)
          No. Keep it. I believe in deciding things
          will be good luck, don't you?

                    NASH
          No. I don't believe in luck.

He tucks the handkerchief back in his pocket, holding her
gaze.

                    NASH (CONT'D)
          But I do believe in assigning value to
          things.

Their faces are close. The moment lingers. That's when Nash
notices the same two Men watching him through the glass door.

                    ALICIA
          Is something wrong?

The MEN spot Nash's look, turn away, begin TALKING. Nash
stares at them a beat longer. Then he looks back at Alicia
and smiles.

                    NASH
          No. Everything's fine.

He begins guiding her away, towards the gardens.

EXT.-GOVERNOR'S MANSION-GARDENS NIGHT-LATER

Nash and Alicia walk the edge of the gardens. Alicia is craning
her neck skyward, towards the glittering canopy of stars.

                    ALICIA
          I once tried to count them all. I
          actually made it to 4,348.

                    NASH
          You are exceptionally odd.

                    ALICIA
          Oh, I bet you're popular with the girls.

                                        (CONTINUED)

CONTINUED:

>          NASH
> Two odd ducks, then.
>          (looking up)
> Pick a shape.

>          ALICIA
> What?

>          NASH
> An animal, anything.

>          ALICIA
> Okay. An...umbrella.

*NASH-POV. As he holds the night in his gaze. The sky grows dark except for a series of stars. They do in fact form an umbrella.*

>          NASH
> Look.

Nash steps behind her, taking her hand in his and guiding her eyes, pointing out the pattern in the stars. Alicia LAUGHS with surprise.

>          ALICIA
> Do it again. Do an octopus.

EXT.-GOVERNOR'S MANSION-NIGHT-WIDE ANGLE-SECONDS LATER

Nash stands with Alicia under a sky totally black save for several glittering constellations. An umbrella. An octopus. A rose.

Two tiny figures in a universe all their own.

EXT.-CAMBRIDGE-BROWNSTONE-SUNSET

A car pulls curbside. Sol emerges.

INT.-BROWNSTONE-SUNSET

Sol KNOCKS on an apartment door. Nothing.

>          SOL
> Nash? Nash?

The door is ajar. Sol pushes into...

INT.-BROWNSTONE-NASH'S APARTMENT-LIVING ROOM-DAY

Small but tasteful. No sign of Nash. (OVER) Sounds from...

INT.-NASH'S APARTMENT-SUN PORCH

Windows face bright rooftops beyond.  Nash sits on the floor
in a sea of magazines, spread out and marked with Nash's
scrawl.

                    SOL
          And I was sure you were house trained.

Nash looks up, startled.

                    NASH
          Do you always just walk into people's
          apartments?

                    SOL
          I'm not going to be the weird one in this
          interaction.

                    NASH
          I'm working.

                    SOL
          And which of our projects involves
          papering your apartment with Life?

                    NASH
          It's classified, Sol.

                    SOL
          I'm serious.  You missed the SAC
          conference today.  The brass were there
          to see you.

                    NASH
          I'm close to something here.

                    SOL
          To what?
               (a beat)
          You skip work.  You miss briefings.  Me
          and Bender, we're worried about you.

Nash has risen, is now taping magazine pages to the wall.
Sol lifts a file of articles off a cabinet.  All on
Hiroshima.

                    SOL (CONT'D)
          We're not doing anything on the Hiroshima
          bomb...

Nash retrieves the file without speaking, deposits it out of
Sol's reach on his desk.

                                        (CONTINUED)

CONTINUED:

> SOL (CONT'D)
> That was polite. `

> NASH
> Did you know the initial blast was so
> bright it left only shadows?

Nash looks at Sol for the first time. His eyes aren't just
tired. They're haunted.

> NASH (CONT'D)
> It seared them on park benches, on
> schoolyards, on sidewalks. They're still
> there.

> SOL
> John...

But Nash just raises his hand.

> NASH
> I'll be back at work tomorrow.

Sol stares as Nash goes to his desk and resumes working.
Finally Sol leaves.

HOLD on Nash as (OVER) the door SHUTS.

DISSOLVE TO:

INT.-NASH'S APARTMENT-SUN PORCH-SUNSET

*Nash is standing over his sea of torn pages. His eyes are red,
tired. All around him shifting patterns rise and fall with ever
increasing speed.*

*Suddenly, the rapid cascade of patterns freezes, leaving a
single pattern.*

Nash goes down on his knees, grabbing his clipboard and, still
staring at the pattern, begins to write furiously.

A SERIES OF CUTS-Nash marking certain words and pictures on
various articles; Nash delineating a route on a paper map of
the U.S.; Nash sliding his work into a Wheeler envelope and
sealing it with wax.

EXT.-CAMBRIDGE STREET-NIGHT

(OVER) CRICKETS. Nash is walking, alone, past large houses set
apart on larger lots, his sealed, grey Wheeler envelope in his
hand.

(CONTINUED)

CONTINUED:


He stops before a giant wrought iron gate, behind which sits a resplendent white colonial mansion.  Lights burn in every room.

On the gate, a small keypad is illuminated by the purple glow of a tiny bulb. Nash stares at the keypad, reaches forward.

NASH'S WRIST-CLOSE. In the purple light, a new set of numbers appear beneath the surface of his skin.

He rubs his wrist in wonder. Then enters the numbers into the keypad. The lock CLICKS open. Nash pushes the gate wide.

EXT.-CAMBRIDGE ESTATE-NIGHT

Beyond the gate is a free standing mailbox. Freshly painted wrought iron secured with a heavy padlock.

Nash slides the gray envelope into the mail slot. (OVER) A sudden RUSTLING from behind him.

Nash spins. Bushes move. Just the wind? (OVER) The HUM of the automatic gate beginning to close. Nash starts to move towards the street.

DOWN THE BLOCK headlights. A car approaches. Nash pins himself behind a tree as the car comes closer.

THE GATE is closing.

THE CAR slows.

NASH-CLOSE watches. Scared. Finally, the car moves off. Nash darts from behind the tree and makes it out through the closing gate at the last possible instant.

EXT.-CAMBRIDGE STREET-NIGHT

Nash moves, first a jog, then a run towards his car parked at the end of the street.

EXT.-WALDEN POND-DAY

A cradle of lush forest. Alicia and John sit over the remains of their picnic.

                    ALICIA
          You don't talk much, do you?

Nash just smiles. The silence stretches on.

                    NASH
          That's novel. I have been told I talk too
          much.

                                        (CONTINUED)

CONTINUED:

                    ALICIA
        No. I mean about, you know, what's really
        going on?

                    NASH
        I can't talk about my work, Alicia.

                    ALICIA
        I don't mean work.

John throws a wry grin.

                    NASH
        I find that polishing my interactions in
        order to make them sociable requires a
        tremendous effort. I have a tendency to
        expedite information flow by being direct.
        Often I don't get a good result.

                    ALICIA
        Try me.

John stares at her a beat. Then...

                    NASH
        All right. I find you attractive. Your
        aggressive moves towards me indicate you
        feel the same way. Still ritual requires
        that we continue a number of platonic
        activities before we can have intercourse.
        I am proceeding with these activities,
        although, to some extent, all I really want
        is to have sex as soon as possible.

Alicia stares at him a beat.

                    NASH (CONT'D)
        Are you going to slap me now?

She leans in and kisses him on the mouth.

                    ALICIA
        How was that result?

EXT.-NASH'S APARTMENT HALLWAY-LIVING ROOM-NIGHT

Dark. The door swings open, flooding the room with yellow hall
light. Alicia stands in the open doorway.

                    NASH
        Wait here a second.

John moves through the living room, hurries into...

INT.-NASH'S APARTMENT-SUN PORCH-NIGHT

John gathers up papers, throws his work into a filing cabinet. He glances out the window.

A black sedan sits parked across the street. Inside, two men. A beat. John draws the shade.

                    ALICIA (OVER)
          Cleaning up your dirty magazines?

John spins. Alicia stands behind him. She's unbuttoning her shirt.

                    NASH
          I told you to wait.

And she peels off her shirt, naked now to her waist.

                    ALICIA
          I couldn't.

Nash moves to her, bodies intertwining there on the desk, under the slatted light spilling in from the street. PAN DOWN...

On the floor are several of John's newspapers, marked up with his code-breaking scrawl. Fallen to the floor. Forgotten.

EXT.-BEACON HILL-DAY

Nash stands atop the hill, looking out at the city beyond.

Suddenly downtown Boston erupts with a low nuclear cloud. Next comes the white light, then the blast wave, leveling buildings, whipping toward Nash in a colossal wave of ruin.

Nash stands, eyes wide, as the wave wipes past him, leveling all in its path but leaving him unscathed.

Nash stands alone, around him only isolation, the last man in a barren desert of twisted buildings and seared shadows.

INT.-NASH'S APARTMENT-BEDROOM-NIGHT

Nash bolts up in his bed, sweating and breathless from the nightmare. He looks at Alicia, asleep peacefully beside him.

EXT.-MIT COMMONS-DAY

Nash sits under a tree, marking up another magazine. A little girl (MARCEE, 6) walks up to him.

CONTINUED:

                    MARCEE
          What ya doin?

Nash looks up at her.

                    NASH
          I am attempting to isolate patterned
          recurrences across periodicals over time.
          And you?

                    MARCEE
          Chasin' pigeons. You talk funny, Mr. Nash.

                    NASH
               (frowning)
          Do I know you?

                    MARCEE
          My uncle says you're very smart but not
          very nice so I shouldn't pay any
          attention if you're mean to me.

                    NASH
          And who might that uncle be?

                    VOICE (OVER)
          The prodigal roommate returns.

Nash looks up and standing over him is Charles. Nash grins.

EXT.-MIT CAMPUS-WALKING

Nash and Charles stroll together. Marcee runs a few yards ahead,
chasing pigeons, eyes wide with a child's fascination.

                    CHARLES
          My sister got herself killed in a car
          crash. Her cowboy husband was too drunk to
          know he was too drunk to drive. I took
          Marcee in.

                    NASH
          She's so small.

                    CHARLES
          She's young. That's how they come.

Marcee runs at the pigeons. To her dismay, they don't react.

                    CHARLES (CONT'D)
          I'm doing the Great Authors Workshop at
          Harvard. D.H. Lawrence.

                                        (CONTINUED)

                    NASH
          You really should buy yourself a new book.

                    CHARLES
          Well, I have been reading about you. How
          are you, John?

                    NASH
          At first all my work was...trivial. Then a
          new assignment came up. ...I can't discuss
          it.

                    CHARLES
          Top Secret, Black Bag, Black Ops?

                    NASH
          Something like that. And....

                    CHARLES
          Yes.

                    NASH
          I've met a girl.

                    CHARLES
          An actual human girl?

                    NASH
          Homo sapien.

                    CHARLES
          Biped?

                    NASH
          And contrary to all probabilities, she
          finds me attractive on a lot of levels.

                    CHARLES
          That's wonderful. Although there's no
          accounting for taste.

                    NASH
          Do I marry her? I mean, it all seems to add
          up. But how do you know for sure?

                    CHARLES
          Nothing's ever for sure. That's the only
          sure thing I know.

That's when Marcee runs up, her expression grave.

                    MARCEE
          I can't make the pigeons fly.

CONTINUED:

                    NASH
          Put your arms up and roar like a monster.

                    MARCEE
          Are you being mean and I shouldn't pay any
          attention to you?

A beat. Then Nash smiles.

EXT.-MIT COMMONS-DAY

Two men and a little girl, arms high, ROARING like monsters,
race through the pigeons, the birds soaring away, taking flight.

INT.-BACK BAY RESTAURANT-NIGHT

Small. Romantic. Alicia sits drinking a beer, staring out at the
river. John arrives at the table, really, really late.

                    NASH
          Alicia, now please don't be angry.

Her look stops him cold. He begins digging in his pockets trying
to find something.

                    NASH (CONT'D)
          I lost track of time at work. Again. I'm
          sorry. I didn't have time to wrap it.

Nash has reached into his pocket, hands her something.

                    NASH (CONT'D)
          Happy Birthday.

Finally she takes the object from John. It's a small glass ball.

                    NASH (CONT'D)
          The refractive faces create a full
          wavelength dispersal so when you look
          inside you get...

                    ALICIA
          Every possible color.

She stares at him, frowning.

                    NASH
          You said God was a painter. At the party?
          Because of all the colors...

                    ALICIA
          I didn't think you were listening.

                                        (CONTINUED)

CONTINUED:

                    NASH
          I'm always listening.

She holds his eyes a beat, realizing. It's the simple truth. She
stares at the object, fractured light hitting her face.

                    ALICIA
          It's so beautiful.

Nash stares. She is. He drops to his knee.

                    NASH
          Alicia, does our relationship warrant long
          term commitment?

She opens her mouth to speak, closes it again.

                    NASH (CONT'D)
          I require a proof. Some kind of
          verifiable empirical data.

Alicia LAUGHS, shakes her head.

                    ALICIA
          Just give me a moment to redefine my
          girlish notions of romance.

Alicia smiles wryly.

                    ALICIA (CONT'D)
          A proof. Verifiable data. All right, how
          big is the universe?

                    NASH
          Infinite.

                    ALICIA
          How do you know?

                    NASH
          I know because all the data indicates that
          it's infinite.

                    ALICIA
          But it hasn't been proven? You haven't seen
          it?

                    NASH
          No.

                    ALICIA
          Then how do you know for sure?

CONTINUED:


               NASH
I don't. I just believe it.

              ALICIA
It's the same with love, I imagine.

Nash stares at her, framed by the window light.

          ALICIA (CONT'D)
The part you don't know. Is if I want to
marry you.

HOLD on Nash. That really hadn't occurred to him. He blanches.

EXT.-WEDDING RECEPTION-WINTER-DAY

Bender, Sol and a few of Alicia's friends hurl rice as John and
Alicia emerge. The couple poses while folks snap pictures.

As Alicia hugs her mother and sister, John notices a figure
standing a few feet off on the edge of the affair. Parcher.

A flash catches John's attention. When he turns back, Parcher is
gone.

EXT.-CAMBRIDGE STREET-NIGHT

NASH'S WRIST-CLOSE. In the glow of the purple light, a new
set of numbers shine through the skin. WIDER.

Nash punches in the codes, pushes open the gate, a new sealed
grey Wheeler envelope in his hand. He drops the envelope into
the slot.

(OVER) A SCREECHING of tires. CAR HEADLIGHTS turn onto the
street. Nash stands frozen, the car bearing down on him.

Suddenly the car SCREECHES to a halt. A figure is SHOUTING from
the driver's seat.

             PARCHER
   In! Fast!

INT.-PARCHER'S CAR-CAMBRIDGE STREET-NIGHT

Parcher GUNS the engine before Nash's door is even closed.

              NASH
What are you doing here?

             PARCHER
Are they following?

                          (CONTINUED)

CONTINUED:


                        NASH
          Who?
              (looking over his shoulder)
          Shit!

OUT THE BACK WINDSCREEN. Another set of headlights SCREECHES
around the corner, in close pursuit.

                        PARCHER
          The drop has been compromised.

(OVER) A sharp CRACK. The back window shatters.

                        PARCHER (CONT'D)
              (shouting)
          Down.

John ducks.  Parcher cuts around the corner, slamming John,
hard, into the car door.

                        PARCHER (CONT'D)
          Take this.

Parcher, still steering with one hand, tosses something onto
the seat.  A revolver.  Nash just stares at him blankly.

                        PARCHER (CONT'D)
          Return fire.

                        NASH
          I don't know how-

                        PARCHER
          Out the window!  Shoot, goddamnit.

EXT.-BOSTON STREETS-NIGHT

The pursuit car is gaining.  A shadowy figure leans out of
the passenger side window, gun in hand.  He FIRES.

INT.-PARCHER'S CAR-BOSTON STREETS-MOVING

(OVER) Another CRACK.  A bullet lodges in the windshield
between Nash and Parcher, spider-webbing the glass.

                        PARCHER
          Shoot the fucking gun.

Nash just stares at the weapon.  Parcher grabs the revolver,
tries steering with one hand and SHOOTING out the window with
the other.

EXT.-BOSTON STREETS-SHORE OF THE CHARLES-NIGHT

Parcher's car turns onto the riverfront, the chase car in
close pursuit.  Parcher and the shadowy gunman exchange FIRE
as the two cars race along the moonlit edge of the Charles.

INT.-PARCHER'S CAR-MOVING

> PARCHER
>Hang on.  I'm going to try and get a
>better shot.

> NASH
>Can't we just get away?

Parcher spins the wheel, hitting the breaks...

EXT. BOSTON STREETS-SHORE OF THE CHARLES-NIGHT

Parcher's car spins broadside.  The pursuit car is bearing
down on them.  Parcher aims out the window and FIRES, SHOT
after SHOT.

The pursuit car keeps coming.  Parcher lets off a final
VOLLEY, the pursuit car now virtually on top of them.

At the last instant, the villains' windshield SHATTERS, the
pursuit car skidding off the road and flying, hard, into the
water.

INT.-PARCHER'S CAR-MOVING

CLOSE on John's eyes.  Wide with disbelief.

EXT.-SHORE OF THE CHARLES-NIGHT

Parcher and Nash emerge from their car, watching as the last
signs of the sedan are swallowed by the black water.

> NASH
>This doesn't happen.  Not here.

> PARCHER
> (adrenalized)
>Yes.  You're right.  It never happened.
>Do you understand me?  It never happened.

Nash nods dumbly.

> PARCHER (CONT'D)
>We have a leak.  They know our operative
>is at Wheeler.  They just don't know who.
>Keep working.  We'll contact you.

(CONTINUED)

CONTINUED:

John manages to nod.

                    PARCHER (CONT'D)
          I've got to get rid of this car.

(OVER) A distant SIREN.  Parcher hands him the gun.

                    PARCHER (CONT'D)
          Keep it.  You may need it.

John looks down at the gun in his hand.  A beat.

EXT.-SHORE OF THE CHARLES-NIGHT-HIGH ANGLE

John watches Parcher's car pull away. Then he hurls the gun into
the dark waters, starts off at a jog, away into the shadows.

INT.-NASH'S APARTMENT-LATE

Nash ENTERS.  The apartment has changed.  A woman's touch.
Alicia is sitting on the couch.

                    ALICIA
          I was worried.

She rushes to her husband, wrapping her arms around him.  But
he stands there, still, like a ghost.

                    ALICIA (CONT'D)
          Sol said you left the office hours ago.
          When you didn't call...
               (pulling back)
          John...?

He just shakes his head.  Kisses her on the cheek distantly.
Then he goes into the study and closes the door.

Alicia stares at the shut door.  Tries the knob.  Locked.

                    ALICIA (CONT'D)
          Baby, what is it?

No answer.  She bows her forehead against the door.

                    ALICIA (CONT'D)
          John, please answer me.  John?

But from beyond the shut portal, only silence.

                    ALICIA (CONT'D)
          What's happened?

Anger turns to rage.

                                              (CONTINUED)

CONTINUED:

                    ALICIA (CONT'D)
        Why won't you talk to me?

She begins banging on the door.

                    ALICIA (CONT'D)
        What's wrong with you, John?  Why don't
        you answer me?

INT.-NASH'S SUN PORCH-NIGHT-CONTINUOUS

Nash leans against the door, Alicia's questions cutting like
wounds.

INT./EXT.-MIT-CLASSROOM-DAY

John stands at the window, staring out at the parking row. A
black sedan pulls up. Two suspicious men in trench coats and
hats emerge.

NASH-CLOSE. Really nervous.

Then two women emerge from the car, followed by their kids. Not
hit men, just two families. WIDER...

John turns to face a classroom full of students, all staring at
him with confusion. His eyes are hollow as he moves to his desk.

                    NASH
        Welcome to section two of advanced
        multivariable calculus.
            (off booklets on his desk)
        Here is the final exam I will be giving in
        ten weeks. Class participation is neither
        expected nor desired. Have a nice day.

Nash walks out, leaving the group of stunned students behind.

INT.-MIT-WHEELER HEADQUARTERS-HALLWAY-DUSK

The setting sun draws long shadows. Nash pulls his office door
closed. He turns, practically colliding with Parcher.

                    NASH
            (jumping back)
        Christ!
            (gathers himself)
        I was just coming to see you. I'm getting
        paranoid. Any time a car backfires-

Parcher's nod seems anything but surprised.

(CONTINUED)

CONTINUED:

                    PARCHER
I understand. Better than you can possibly
imagine.

                    NASH
I can't keep doing this.

William's eyes seem terribly sad. He leads John back into...

INT.-NASH'S OFFICE-SUNSET

Dark. Shades drawn.

                    PARCHER
You need to calm down, John.

Parcher leads John to a chair, then sits across from him.

                    PARCHER (CONT'D)
Great deeds come at great cost. Your words,
John.  We're closing in on the bomb, in
large part due to your work. Isn't your
fear a small price to pay?

                    NASH
My situation has changed.  I have just
found out Alicia is pregnant.

                    PARCHER
I told you attachments were dangerous. You
chose to marry the girl. I did nothing to
prevent it. Don't make me regret that.

                    NASH
What do you mean, prevent it?

William's answer is only silence.

                    PARCHER
The best way to insure everyone's safety is
to continue your work.

                    NASH
That's bullshit. I'll just quit.

                    PARCHER
No. You won't.

                    NASH
Why the hell not?

(CONTINUED)

CONTINUED:

                     PARCHER
         Because I keep the Russians from knowing
         you work for us.

It's finally now when John realizes what's wrong with
Parcher's eyes.  They're dead.

                PARCHER (CONT'D)
         If you quit working for me, I quit working
         for you.

In the dying light, William turns, heads out the door.

INT.-MIT-WHEELER HEADQUARTERS-HALLWAY-CONTINUOUS

Nash emerges a beat later, shaking off the shock.

                   NASH
                (shouting)
         Parcher! PARCHER!

Sol emerges from his door, stares at Nash, obviously concerned.

                   SOL
         You okay? Who are you shouting at?

But Nash doesn't answer, just stares after Parcher as the front
door kisses closed behind him.

INT.-NASH'S APARTMENT-SUN PORCH-LATE NIGHT

Nash sits, his back to us, in the dark, peeking through the
blinds. Alicia ENTERS.

                 ALICIA (OVER)
     John?

Alicia flicks on the light, standing now in the doorway.

                   NASH
                (spinning)
         Turn it off.

We see his face now, unshaven, cheeks hollow, eyes wide.

                 NASH (CONT'D)
                (shouting)
         Turn off the light.

He is up, lamp SMASHING into the wall.

                                (CONTINUED)

CONTINUED:

                    NASH (CONT'D)
          Why would you do that? Why would you turn
          the light on?

Alicia's hand has moved to her stomach.

                    ALICIA
          What's wrong with you?

John stares at her another beat. Then he turns and peeks
through one of the blinds.

                    NASH
          They're out there.

OUT THE WINDOW. A black sedan. An identical car pulls up beside
it. A shadow inside the first car points towards John's
apartment.

                    ALICIA
               (moving towards the window)
          Who's out there?

But John moves forward, blocks her way with his arm.

                    NASH
          They don't necessarily know you're here.

                    ALICIA
          Who? What are you talking about?

John just stares at her. When his VOICE comes, it's soft.

                    NASH
          Go to your sister's. I left the car around
          back. Take Commonwealth Avenue. No side
          streets, stay where it's crowded. Go to
          your sister's, wait for me to call you.

                    ALICIA
          John, what's going on? Please, you've got
          to talk to me-

                    NASH
               (exploding)
          Go. Now. GET OUT! GO!

Alicia takes an involuntary step backwards, and John SLAMS the
door. Then he goes back to the window.

INT.-NASH'S BEDROOM-CONTINUOUS

HOLD on Alicia, expression indecipherable. Too much time passes.

                                              (CONTINUED)

CONTINUED:


Then she goes to the phone and lifts the receiver.

EXT.-HARVARD UNIVERSITY-DAY

Nash climbs the steep steps of the Mathematics Quad. His suit looks slept in. He keeps glancing behind him.

                    MARCEE (OVER)
          Mean Uncle John, Mean Uncle John.

A small, familiar figure runs up to greet him. She raises her hands high over her head, bares her teeth and looses a savage GROWL.

                    MARCEE (CONT'D)
          See, I remembered.

                    NASH
          You sure did.

He lifts her up in his arms and hugs her, tight, eyes closing against the smell of her small girl's hair. Sets her down.

                    CHARLES
          Someone really needed a hug.
               (clasps John's hand)
          Saw you on the slate. Couldn't miss hearing
          a guest lecture by the inimitable John
          Nash.

Nash's smile is weak.

                    CHARLES (CONT'D)
          What is it? What's wrong?

                    NASH
          I'm into something. ...I need help.

                    CHARLES
               (darkening)
          What? Tell me...

John looks like he's about to speak. Then...

                    VOICE (OVER)
          Professor Nash...

A GRADUATE STUDENT is crossing the courtyard, beckoning him towards the open door of the main mathematics building.

                    NASH
          We'll talk after. Okay?

                                        (CONTINUED)

CONTINUED:


Before Charles can stop him, Nash heads inside.

INT.-HARVARD-LECTURE HALL

John stands on stage, a blackboard scrawled with numbers behind
him. He is speaking, staring out into the audience.

>           NASH
>      ...And so we see that if the zeroes of the
>      Riemann zeta function correspond to
>      singularities in space time then
>      conventional number theory breaks down in
>      the face of relativistic exploration...

Nash's VOICE trails off. A couple of MEN have ENTERED the upper
balcony, wearing overcoats and hats.

>           NASH (CONT'D)
>      Sometimes, our expectations are betrayed by
>      the numbers...

Another MAN has emerged at the top of the center aisle, also in
overcoat and top hat.

>           NASH (CONT'D)
>      And variables are impossible to assign any
>      rational value...

Nash has moved forward to the Graduate Student in the front row.

>           NASH (CONT'D)
>      Is there another way out of here?

The student, confused, points to a side door. Nash turns and
rushes off stage. The audience stares in befuddled wonder.

EXT.-HARVARD MATHEMATICS QUAD-HIGH ANGLE

Nash races across the quad, evading two Men in overcoats who
burst from the building, giving chase.

EXT.-HARVARD MATHEMATICS QUAD-DAY

Nash is running down the main steps when another Man appears at
the base of the stairway, blocking his way. Nash stops cold.

>           MAN
>      Professor Nash.

Nash spins. One of the Men from the lecture hall is descending
the steps towards Nash. Nowhere to run.

CONTINUED:

                    MAN (CONT'D)
          Let's avoid a scene, shall we?

                    NASH
          What do you want?

                    MAN
          My name is Dr. Rosen. I'm a psychiatrist.

                    NASH
          You will forgive me if I don't seem
          persuaded.

                    ROSEN
          I'd like you to come with me, John. Just
          for a chat.

                    NASH
          And if I say no?

                    ROSEN
          I have a court order signed by a judge. I
          hope we can proceed without any
          unpleasantness.

He continues down towards Nash. John offers a charming smile.

                    NASH
          Well I suppose I don't have much choice.

That's when John hauls off and DECKS him, hard, across the face.
Bolts towards the street.

The other men are on him in a second. One grabs him, taking Nash
rolling down the cement steps before restraining him.

                    NASH (CONT'D)
          Get away from me. Don't you think I know
          who you are?

Rosen approaches, pulling a hypo from a case in his coat.

                    NASH (CONT'D)
                    (shouting)
          Somebody! Stop them!

People are watching. At the top of the steps, Charles and Marcee
have emerged. John spots them.

                    NASH (CONT'D)
          Charles. Help me.  They're Russians.

That's when Rosen sinks the needle into his arm.

                                              (CONTINUED)

CONTINUED:

                    ROSEN
                 (gentle)
        There now. All better.

Nash's struggling begins to slow as the medication takes effect.

                  ROSEN (CONT'D)
              (to the crowd)
       Everything's all right here.

The two Men stuff John into the back of the car as Rosen climbs in next to the driver.

INT.-SEDAN-MOVING

Nash stares out the window at Charles coming fast down the steps, Marcee behind him.

Nash raises his hand towards his friend, finding only window glass between them as the car pulls away, leaving the university behind.

                               CUT TO:

INT.-OFFICE-EVENING

NASH-POV. DARKNESS. Then light through the blinks of slowly opening eyes reveal Rosen's peering face.

                  ROSEN
     John...

Nash lays on a couch, Rosen sitting over him. Leather chairs, an oak desk, degrees on the walls. Picture perfect.

                  ROSEN (CONT'D)
     John, can you hear me?

Nash blinks. Takes in Rosen. Tries to sit up. No luck. He looks down. His hands are bound.

                  ROSEN (CONT'D)
     Go easy. The Thorazine takes a little while
     to wear off.
         (off John's hands)
     I'm sorry about the restraints. But...
         (rubs his chin)
     You have a hell of a right hook.

                  NASH
     Where am I?

                           (CONTINUED)

CONTINUED:

              ROSEN
    Macarthur Psychiatric Hospital.

              NASH
    I find that highly unlikely.

              ROSEN
    Who do you think I am, John?

John stares at him a beat.

              ROSEN (CONT'D)
    At Harvard, you said I was Russian. What
    did you mean by that?

              NASH
    This is a mistake. My work is nonmilitary
    in application.

              ROSEN
    What work is that, John?

              NASH
    I don't know anything, alright?

Rosen's smile is just a little too kind.

              ROSEN
    There's no good in keeping secrets.

John jumps up, tries for the door. But he goes down, hard.
His ankles have restraints around them too.

John looks up from the floor. What he sees chills his bones.
Sitting on a window seat in the corner is a single figure.
Charles, staring at him sadly.

              NASH
    Charles?

But his old friend says nothing, just sits there. Rosen has gone
to the desk and pressed a buzzer.

              NASH (CONT'D)
      (shouting)
    The prodigal roommate revealed! Saw my
    name on the lecture slate? You lying son
    of a bitch! How do you say Charles Herman
    in Russian?

Charles remains silent. Rosen stares at Nash a beat.

                            (CONTINUED)

CONTINUED:

                  ROSEN
         Who are you talking to, John?  There's no
         one there.

Two burly orderlies ENTER.

                  NASH
         What are you talking about? He's right
         there.

Rosen nods and the orderlies begin dragging him out the door.

                  NASH (CONT'D)
         Stop. I don't know anything. Where are you
         taking me? Stop!

INT.-HALLWAY-CONTINUOUS

The orderlies are dragging John down the hallway.

                  NASH
         My name is John Nash. I am being held
         against my will. Somebody contact the
         Department of Defense.

Charles stares at him sadly from the doorway.

                  NASH (CONT'D)
         My name is John Nash. I am being held
         against my will. Somebody contact the
         Department of Defense.

And he is gone, pulled into the shadows and out of sight.

EXT.-MACARTHUR HOSPITAL-DAY

Steepled brick buildings situated on resplendent browning lawns.
Folks wander like ghosts. A sprawling palace of the mad.

INT.-MACARTHUR HOSPITAL CELL-DAY

John Nash sits on a cot in a cell, rocking. PULL BACK...

INT.-MACARTHUR HOSPITAL-HALLWAY

Alicia stands watching John through the window of his cell. She
turns now, eyes red, to face Rosen.

                  ALICIA
         What's wrong with him?

CONTINUED:

                    ROSEN
          John has schizophrenia. He has lost his
          ability to tell the difference between what
          is real and what is imagined.

Rosen shuts the sliding viewport on Nash's cell door.

                    ROSEN (CONT'D)
          People with this disorder are often
          paranoid.

                    ALICIA
          But John's work... He deals with
          conspiracies.

                    ROSEN
          Seeing conspiracies, finding hidden codes,
          these are the hallmarks of the illness.

                    ALICIA
          No, no. That's what he does-

                    ROSEN
          Yes. In John's world, these behaviors are
          accepted, encouraged. As such, his illness
          may have gone untreated longer than is
          typical.

                    ALICIA
          What do you mean? How long?

Rosen takes a beat, begins walking her down the hallway.

                    ROSEN
          Possibly since graduate school. At least
          that's when his hallucinations seem to have
          begun.

                    ALICIA
          What are you talking about? What
          hallucinations?

                    ROSEN
          One, so far, that I am aware of. An
          imaginary roommate named Charles Herman.

Alicia looks at Rosen like he's the crazy one.

                    ALICIA
          Charles isn't imaginary. He and John have
          been best friends since Princeton.

(CONTINUED)

CONTINUED:

                       ROSEN
Have you ever met Charles?

Rosen holds her gaze, watches her glimpse then discard the
panic.

                       ROSEN (CONT'D)
Has he ever come to dinner?

                       ALICIA
He's always in town for so little time.
Lecturing.

                       ROSEN
Was he at your wedding?

                       ALICIA
He had to teach.

                       ROSEN
Have you ever seen a picture of him? Have
you ever spoken with him on the phone?

                       ALICIA
...This is ridiculous.

But her words carry more conviction than her eyes.

                       ROSEN
I phoned Princeton. According to housing
records John lived alone.

                       ALICIA
There's probably just a clerical error at
Princeton.

                       ROSEN
Alicia, I was with John when he saw
Charles. There was no one there.

                       ALICIA
This is absurd.

                       ROSEN
Which is more likely, that your husband, a
mathematician with no military training, is
a government spy fleeing the Russians...

                       ALICIA
You're making him sound crazy-

                       ROSEN
...Or that he has lost his grip on reality?

CONTINUED:


Alicia starts to speak. Then purses her lips, not sure what to
say.

                    ROSEN (CONT'D)
          The only way I can help John is to show him
          the difference between what is real and
          what is in his mind.

                    ALICIA
          What John does is classified.

                    ROSEN
          He mentioned a supervisor at Wheeler.
          William Parcher. Maybe he can clarify
          things for us. But I can't get to him
          without clearances.

Alicia stops, eyes narrowing with suspicion.

                    ALICIA
          You want me to help you get the details of
          my husband's work?

Rosen's sudden smile seems forced.

                    ROSEN
          John thinks I'm a Russian spy. Is that what
          you think?

Alicia is silent. Holds Rosen's eyes.

                    ROSEN (CONT'D)
          You called me, Alicia. You knew something
          was wrong.

                    ALICIA
          He wasn't sleeping. I wanted someone to
          talk with him. Bender recommend-

                    ROSEN
          So your Mr. Bender, is he part of this
          conspiracy as well?

Alicia stares at him a beat. Unsure. Then...

                    ALICIA
          This was all a mistake. He's just over-
          tired. I'll take him home now.

                    ROSEN
          Alicia, no one wants someone they love to
          be sick.

                                        (CONTINUED)

CONTINUED:

                    ALICIA
          What I want is my husband released.

She's growing agitated. Rosen's smile is full of compassion.

                    ROSEN
          John's been given something to sleep. Come
          back in the morning. Nine AM-.

                    ALICIA
          I'm not leaving him here.

                    ROSEN
          He attacked me. I've committed him
          Alicia. It's not up to you anymore.

She stares at him, fighting back the fear.

                    ROSEN (CONT'D)
          After you've had a good night's rest, if we
          still can't agree on what's best for John
          I'll release him into your custody.

Alicia stares at him. Nowhere to go. Finally...

                    ALICIA
          Nine. And I want him ready to leave.

And with that she walks off. HOLD on Rosen as he watches her go.

EXT.-NASH APARTMENT-NIGHT

Dark. A light burns in the office window.

INT.-NASH APARTMENT-OFFICE-NIGHT

Alicia is rifling through John's desk. She finds his address
book in a drawer. Opens it to Charles Herman's phone number.

Alicia reaches for the phone and dials the number. (OVER) The
RING signal CLICKS.

                    OPERATOR
          This is the operator. You are calling a non-
          working number.

HOLD an Alicia's face. Eyes hollow, like a ghost's.

EXT.-MIT-WHEELER COMPOUND-MORNING-LONG SHOT

Alicia stands at the guard booth. Sol and Bender run up to greet
her, clearing the guard to raise the barricade.

EXT.-MIT-WHEELER HEADQUARTERS-MORNING

Alicia is moving towards the main building, a woman on a
mission, Sol and Bender trailing behind.

>                    BENDER
>           What did the Doctor say?

>                    SOL
>           Is he sick?

>                    ALICIA
>           I need to know what John's been working on.

>                    SOL
>           Alicia, you can't go in there.

>                    BENDER
>           You know it's classified. Alicia. Stop.

What she does now is extraordinary. She SLAPS him across the
face. Alicia and Bender stand staring at each other, stunned.

INT.-MIT-WHEELER-NASH'S OFFICE-MOMENTS LATER

Sol pushes open the door. The walls, ceiling and windows are
covered with scrawled magazine and newspaper clippings. The
work is, without question, bizarre, perhaps even mad.

>                    ALICIA
>           Oh my God.

INT. MIT-WHEELER-NASH'S OFFICE-MOMENTS LATER

Alicia moves along the wall, staring at John's work.

>                    ALICIA
>           Why didn't you say something? I mean, all
>           this...

>                    SOL
>           John's always been, you know, weird.

>                    BENDER
>           He said he was doing code breaking. That it
>           was eyes only.

>                    SOL
>           Top secret. Part of the military effort.

>                    ALICIA
>           Was he?

(CONTINUED)

CONTINUED:

     SOL
It's possible. Directives come down all the
time that some of us aren't cleared for. It
was possible.

     BENDER
Possible. But not likely. Lately he's
seemed more and more agitated. Then you
called...

     ALICIA
So this is all he's been doing every day?
Cutting up magazines.

Sol and Bender exchange a look.

     SOL
Not exactly all.

EXT.-MIT-WHEELER COMPOUND-WALKING-DAY

Bender, Alicia and Sol walk the row of abandoned warehouses.

     SOL
He keeps coming down here.

     BENDER
We figured he was thinking.

     SOL
He used to do that a lot at school.

     BENDER
Ride his bike in figure eights.

     SOL
Just thinking.

PULL BACK TO REVEAL...The three of them face the warehouse
that housed William's secret lab. No armed guard. Alicia
pushes inside.

INT.-WAREHOUSE-DAY

No secret lab. No personnel. Just sunlight painting the dust
through the windows. PULL BACK as Alicia stands alone in the
giant, empty space.

     BENDER
He's been going in here. You hear him
sort of...talking to himself.

         (CONTINUED)

CONTINUED:

                    ALICIA
                 (turning)
       I need John's supervisor. I need to talk to
       William Parcher.

SOL-CLOSE. His frown is inscrutable.

EXT.-MACARTHUR-GARDENS-MORNING-WALKING

Crisp. Sunny. John alternately paces and stares out at the
hills beyond. His hands are bound. A burly Orderly stands
sentry a few feet behind.

                   ROSEN (OVER)
       How are you this morning, John?

John turns to face Rosen. All around them, patients mill.

                   NASH
       Well it seems obvious by now that you're
       not going to kill me. You can imagine
       that's a load off my mind.

Rosen can't help but smile.

                   ROSEN
       You still think I'm a Russian spy?

                   NASH
       You still want to pretend you're not?

                   ROSEN
       You are a rational man. Let me appeal to
       your rationality. Why do you think I didn't
       see Charles in my office?

                   NASH
       I think you did see him. I think you're
       trying to drive me into some kind of
       nervous breakdown.

                   ROSEN
       And why would I want to do that?

                   NASH
       To find out if I know anything.

Rosen nods. He doesn't seem surprised.

                   ROSEN
       So Charles, is he a conspirator too?

                                    (CONTINUED)

CONTINUED:

                    NASH
          Maybe you forced him to cooperate. Maybe
          you threatened Marcee.

                    ROSEN
          Marcee? Who is Marcee, John?

                    NASH
          I am not moved by your feigned ignorance.

Rosen just smiles, shakes his head.

                    ROSEN
          And your wife. She phoned me. Is she part
          of this also?

John stumbles a beat. Then recovers.

                    NASH
          She's confused.

                    ROSEN
          Is she, John? Or is it possible that you're
          confused?
               (a beat)
          Look at Mr. Engle over there...

Rosen motions across the courtyard. A white haired man stands in
a corner, gesturing angrily, TALKING to thin air.

                    ROSEN (OVER) (CONT'D)
          For years people have referred to madness
          as being without reason. But that isn't
          true. That fellow is as reasonable as you
          or I.

The white haired man begins to plead and SHOUT.

                    ROSEN (OVER) (CONT'D)
          We simply cannot see his reason. We cannot
          see the invisible adversary who makes him
          so angry. But he can, as clear as he sees
          you or me.

Rosen stops, puts his hand on John's arm.

                    ROSEN (CONT'D)
          Look back on the times with Charles and
          Marcee.

                    NASH
          I will not play this game with you.

                                        (CONTINUED)

CONTINUED:

                    ROSEN
          Is it possible that, like him, you were
          really alone?

                    NASH
          I will not indulge this.

                    ROSEN
          John, insulin shock has been known to
          reduce delusions.

John stops, anger flashing in his eyes.

                    NASH
          The other shoe falls. What do you want to
          give me? Sodium pentothal?

                    ROSEN
          Just insulin-

John knocks Rosen's hand away with his bound wrists. Despite his
spiking temper, John seems almost relieved.

                    NASH
          Nastrovia, Comrade Rosen. I told you, I
          don't know anything.
               (voice rising)
          But if this means an end to this goddamned
          charade, then come on. Drug me.

The Orderly has moved in. John spins to face the man.

                    NASH (CONT'D)
          Come on!

But Rosen stops the Orderly with a gesture. Turns to face Nash.

                    ROSEN
          There's no plot against you, John. You're
          going to have to accept that. I won't force
          treatment on you. Let's take you back to
          your room now.

This turn seems to throw John. His expression darkens.

                    NASH
          This is insane.

Rosen's expression is sad.

                    ROSEN
          Yes, John. I'm afraid it is.

EXT.-CAMBRIDGE STREET-DAY

Alicia is walking up a familiar street. She stops, looks up.

EXT.-CAMBRIDGE STREET-MANSION-DAY

The same house we've seen before. And terribly different. Broken
windows. Dilapidated side boards. Long ago deserted.

Alicia walks to the front gate. The remains of an aging lock pad
hangs by wires. Broken. She pushes the gate, CREAKING, open.

EXT.-CAMBRIDGE MANSION-DAY

An old mailbox sits ahead. A rusting pad lock hangs at its base.

Alicia looks up at the empty house. Then she lifts a large
rock and begins HAMMERING away at the lock, face determined.

INT.-MACARTHUR-COMMON ROOM-EVENING

Alicia sits alone, uncomfortable. Other patients at other long
tables. Vacant stares. Alicia's eyes go to an opening door.

John ENTERS, escorted by two orderlies. He sits at the table
across from her. The orderlies retire to a table not far off.

Alicia reaches across and takes his hands, holds them in hers.
The pain on her face is palpable.

                    ALICIA
          John, I'm so sorry.

                    NASH
               (nodding)
          I've been thinking about it. Of course I
          must have looked mad to you. What choice
          did you have?  But I can explain, now.

                    ALICIA
          I was so worried.

                    NASH
          It's going to be all right. But we have to
          speak quietly. They may be listening. There
          may be microphones.

Alicia bites her lip, tries not to react.

                    NASH (CONT'D)
          I'm going to tell you everything, now. I'm
          breaking protocol. But you've got to know.
          You've got to help me get out of here.
               (MORE)

                                        (CONTINUED)

CONTINUED:

                      NASH (CONT'D)
                  (a beat)
          I've been doing top secret work for the
          government. There's a threat of
          catastrophic proportions... I think the
          Reds must believe I'm too high profile to
          simply do away with. So they're trying to
          keep me here. So I can't do my work.

Alicia is staring at him, fighting back the tears.

                      NASH (CONT'D)
          Go to Wheeler. Get in touch with William
          Parcher. He can-(help us).

                      ALICIA
                  (too loud)
          Stop! Just stop!

Folks in the room stare. Nash sits back, stunned. Alicia gathers
herself. Takes a breath.

                      ALICIA (CONT'D)
          John, I've been to Wheeler.

                      NASH
          Good, good-

                      ALICIA
          There is no William Parcher.

                      NASH
          Of course there is. I've been working for
          him-.

                      ALICIA
          Doing what, John? Breaking codes? Dropping
          them in a secret mailbox for the government
          to pick up.

                      NASH
          How could you know that?

                      ALICIA
          Sol followed you one night. He thought it
          was harmless.  Good old Sol.

Alicia has reached into her bag. Lifts something onto the table.

                      ALICIA (CONT'D)
          None of it's been real, John.

And with that, she deposits on the table a stack of gray Wheeler
envelopes. All still sealed with John's seal.

                                              (CONTINUED)

CONTINUED:


                        ALICIA (CONT'D)
                They've never been opened.

John tears one open. Inside, his magazine pages. His marked
maps. Never picked up. Never seen by anyone.

                        ALICIA (CONT'D)
                There is no William Parcher. There is no
                conspiracy. It's all in your mind. You're
                sick, John. Don't you understand, you're
                sick.

Alicia begins to cry, the tears coming now, streaming down her
cheeks. Finally she bows to John's hand on the table, pressing
her cheek to the back of his palm, body racked with trembling
SOBS.

John looks from his weeping wife to his work. He lifts a torn
magazine page, marked and scrawled.

HOLD on John. On his face, for the first time, fear.

INT.-MACARTHUR-CORRIDOR-NIGHT

Rosen is making evening rounds. A NURSE races up to him.

                        NURSE
                Doctor. It's Nash. Code red.

Rosen is on the move, fast.

INT.-MACARTHUR-NASH'S CELL-NIGHT

Rosen UNLOCKS Nash's cell and ENTERS to find Nash, his back to
the door, standing in a pool of blood.

                        ROSEN
                John?

Nash turns, holding his wrist in his hand. Blood is spilling
through his fingers.

As Rosen gently takes John's wrist, he notices the fingernails
of John's other hand. Broken and bloody.

                        NASH
                There's nothing there.

The flesh on top of John's wrist has been gouged away by his own
nails. An Orderly hands Rosen a wad of gauze. Rosen begins to
dress the wound. John's eyes are unblinking, shocky.


                                              (CONTINUED)

CONTINUED:

                         NASH (CONT'D)
              There's no implant. There's nothing there.

INT.-MACARTHUR-TREATMENT ROOM-DAY

Small. A single gurney sits in the middle of the floor. A NURSE
stands by a silver medical table.

The door opens. Nash shuffles in wearing hospital clothes and
paper slippers. He sits on the gurney. Draws up his legs.

INT.-MACARTHUR-OBSERVATION ROOM-DAY

Rosen and Alicia watch through a plexi window.

                         ROSEN
                   This, right now, this is the final
                   nightmare of schizophrenia. THe horror of
                   not knowing what is true...

Leather restraints are pulled tight around his wrists and
ankles, his forehead.

                         ROSEN (CONT'D)
                   Imagine if you suddenly learned that the
                   people, the places, the moments most
                   important to you were not gone, not dead,
                   no, worse, had never been.

The Nurse places a plastic bit in his mouth. Lifts a hypo.

                         ROSEN (CONT'D)
                   What kind of hell would that be?

Alicia touches the divide as the Nurse looks to Rosen for the
nod. She puts the sedative needle to flesh.

Alicia turns away.

INT.-TREATMENT ROOM-SERIES OF SHOTS

The nurse checks Nash's pupil response...Nash's unconscious
body arches into the agony of a Grand Mal seizure...A tube is
slid into Nash's nose, pumping sugar water into his
stomach...Nash comes to, trembling, packed in ice, skin going
blue, as we PULL BACK AND UP...

EXT.-PRINCETON CAMPUS-SPRING-1956

Trees alive with the lush green of spring. Alicia and Sol
walk the familiar paths of campus, pushing a stroller. Alicia
seems older. It's her eyes.

                                              (CONTINUED)

CONTINUED:

                    ALICIA
         Two a week.  For six months.  The
         treatments were...difficult.

                    SOL
         But he's better?

                    ALICIA
                  (reciting)
         Schizophrenia has no cure.  But with
         medication and a low stress environment
         the patient can hope to approximate a
         normal life.  The doctor thought a change
         of scenery.  Somewhere peaceful.  After
         Wheeler terminated his contract-

                    SOL
         Bender and I tried to help keep him on-

Alicia stills him with a casual wave of her hand. She has about
her the odd self-possession that comes with close proximity to
madness.

                    ALICIA
         You can't very well have a lunatic keeping
         government secrets, can you?

She looks off, gaze going well past the visible horizon.

                    ALICIA (CONT'D)
         I found a job at Xerox. R&D. It's not much.
         But John always spoke so fondly of being
         here at Princeton. And Hansen's running the
         department now.

                    SOL
         So he keeps reminding us.

                    ALICIA
         But John won't come near campus. He's
         so...ashamed.

                    SOL
         Alicia, how are you?

                    ALICIA
         The delusions have passed. It's like
         looking at pictures of the Jews from
         Europe. They have this look in their eyes.
         Hard and stunned at the same time. Like
         there's this an entire world stolen out
         from under them. That's the way it is with
         John too, I think. Lost.

                                        (CONTINUED)

CONTINUED:


There is definitely about her an odd feeling, both strong and
fragile, like giant plates of shifting ice.

                    SOL
          No, Alicia. How are **you**?

She seems not to be able to even understand the question.
Then...

                    ALICIA
          You know Heisenberg's uncertainty
          principle? The properties of the object are
          influenced by the observer.

                    SOL
          Yes, I'm familiar with it.

                    ALICIA
          Often what I feel is obligation, or guilt
          over wanting to leave, or rage, against
          John, against God. But then I look at him
          and I force myself to see the man I
          married. And he becomes that man. He's
          transformed into someone I love. And then
          I'm transformed into someone who loves him.
          It's not all the time. But it's enough.

Sol smiles, amazed at this woman.

                    SOL
          John is a lucky man.

                    ALICIA
          And so unlucky.

EXT.-PRINCETON HOUSE-DAY

Sol helps Alicia with the baby as they enter a modest white
colonial.

                    ALICIA
          John, you've got a visitor.

EXT.-PRINCETON HOUSE-DAY

Nash sits on the porch of a modest white colonial, working
over a pad of equations, smoking a cigarette. Sol and Alicia
enter. Alicia kisses John on the head and moves into the
house with the baby.

                    SOL
          Hey, Chief.

                                        (CONTINUED)

CONTINUED:


Nash looks up. He seems pale, drawn, as if part of him has gone missing, been replaced by shadow.

                    NASH
          Finally. A little respect.

Nash offers Sol a cigarette from his pack.

                    SOL
          I quit.

Sol begins to sit in an empty chair.

                    NASH
          Have you said hello to Harvey?

                    SOL
          John, I-

                    NASH
          Relax. What good's being nuts if you can't
          have a little fun?

                    SOL
          Jesus, John.

Alicia emerges. She places two pills and a glass of water on the table.

                    NASH
              (embarrassed)
          I can take those later-

                    ALICIA
              (brave smile)
          You're supposed to take them now.

A beat. Then, humiliated, John swallows his medication. Alicia heads back into the house. Sol watches her go.

                    SOL
          I was in town giving a workshop. Bender
          wanted to come see you but...

                    NASH
          Squeamish?
              (off Sol's shrug)
          I suppose I would be too. But alas, I am
          stuck with me.

Sol gives a sad smile.


                                              (CONTINUED)

CONTINUED:

                    SOL
             I've missed you, John.

Nash seems sincerely puzzled.

                   NASH
            Why?

Sol finds his answer blocked by a lump in his throat, looks
away.

                    SOL
            I thought you might want to take a drive
            into town, get some chinese...

                   NASH
            No, no.
              (a beat)
            I have been working on solving the Riemann
            Hypothesis...

Nash slides his pad over to Sol, his eyes sad.

                 NASH (CONT'D)
            I figured, if I dazzle them, they'd have to
            reinstate me. But the medication makes me
            blurry. I can't see...(the solutions).

Sol's nod is as sad as it is brave. Nash's calculations don't
make much sense. He slides back the pad.

                    SOL
            Go easy. There are other things beside
            work.

John stares at him.

                   NASH
            What are they?

INT.-NASH HOUSE-KITCHEN-NIGHT

Alicia is doing the dishes. John stands staring at the kitchen
table. He lifts a napkin, toys with it curiously, like an alien
come to Earth for the first time.

                   NASH
            What do people do?

By Alicia's expression, this question is not coming for the
first time. But she rallies herself again for the answer.

                             (CONTINUED)

CONTINUED:

                  ALICIA
This. Just this.
       (smiles)
No conspiracies. No earth shattering
discoveries. Just this.

                  NASH
Everything is so meaningless.

                  ALICIA
It's life, John. Activities available.
Just add meaning.

John nods, but by his expression, he surely doesn't understand.

                  ALICIA (CONT'D)
You could try leaving the house. Maybe talk
to people.

He stares at her. The idea is just too daunting.

                  ALICIA (CONT'D)
You could take out the garbage.

                  NASH
       (smiles)
World famous mathematician turned
schizophrenic takes out trash. Now that's
something.

                  ALICIA
There you go. Onward and upward.

He lifts the trash bag, walks out the kitchen door. Alicia
begins putting the dishes away. (OVER) We hear Nash TALKING.

ALICIA-CLOSE. Terrified. She spins as John re-enters.

                  ALICIA (CONT'D)
Who were you talking to?

                  NASH
The garbage man.

                  ALICIA
Garbage men don't come at night.

                  NASH
I guess here they do.

Alicia stares at him. Unsure. Then a figure passes the window. A
garbage man after all, throwing the bag into a truck HISSING
past.

                                (CONTINUED)

CONTINUED:

> ALICIA
>> John, I'm—

He takes her in his arms. She folds into his chest. Normal life has become a mine field.

> NASH
>> It's all right. Everything's going to be all right.

But by his expression, he seems anything but sure.

INT.-NASH LIVING ROOM-AFTERNOON

John stands paralysed, his SCREAMING baby in his arms. He seems entirely unable to handle this unwieldy little human.

Alicia ENTERS, pissed. She scoops up her child in one hand, retrieves the fallen pacifier from the floor with the other.

She feeds their son the binky, the child's CRIES instantly stilled.

Alicia exits with the baby. John stands in the middle of the room, sad, helpless. No good at real life.

INT.-NASH BEDROOM-NIGHT

John lays on his back, Alicia curled beside him. Spring moonlight pours in through the open window.

Alicia kisses his neck tentatively, then his face. John lies still as a statue. He tilts his head away, strokes her head platonically.

> NASH
>> I'm sorry.

HOLD on her face, sad eyes open in the moonlight. A beat. Then she rises, moving into...

INT.-NASH BATHROOM-NIGHT-CONTINUOUS

Alicia goes to the sink, splashes her face. Stares at John's medication bottle on the edge of the basin.

A beat. Then she smashes the mirror with her hand, glass SHATTERING into cracked fragments of loss.

Alicia drops her head as she begins to CRY.

INT.-NASH BEDROOM-NIGHT-CONTINUOUS

John lays in his bed. (OVER) Alicia's SOBS. John curls up in a fetal position. Helpless.

EXT.-NASH HOUSE-NEXT MORNING

John is pouring the shards of the mirror off an impromptu cardboard dustpan into the trash. Alicia emerges from the house, baby in her arms, their brittle dance of normalcy resumed.

> ALICIA
> My mother's going to keep the baby a
> little longer today. I can get three
> hours of overtime.

And before he has a chance to respond, she is gone. Nash stares after his wife, then heads back inside the house.

INT.-NASH HOUSE-SUN PORCH-NIGHT-DAYS LATER

Glass enclosed. Moonlight beams in through the large windows, illuminating the dark forest beyond the lawn. John sits at his desk.

> ALICIA (OVER)
> I'm going to bed.

Alicia sets his medication and water before him. The tension between them is palpable.

> ALICIA (CONT'D)
> Eat up.

> NASH
> Goodnight.

But she is already gone. He stares down at his medication. A beat. Then he opens a cigar box on his desk.

INSIDE THE BOX. Maybe five days worth of his pills. Not taken. John drops the two new tablets inside. Closes the box.

Nash looks at his desk. Piles of unopened mail. Several math journals. He notices a New York Times. He opens the paper.

NASH-POV. *Columns of articles. Suddenly the text goes black, characters rising into the air in a perfectly revealed pattern.*

He slides a pad in front of him, stares at the blank page. (OVER) A RAP as something hits the window. Hard.

(CONTINUED)

CONTINUED:

John peers out into the night. Someone, a silhouette, darts across the lawn. John is up, fast, moving into the hallway.

EXT.-NASH HOUSE-NIGHT-CONTINUOUS

Nash shoves open the screen door, stares out into the night.

                    NASH
          Who's there? Hello?

(OVER) CRICKETS. A figure bolts across the green, little more than a shadow, racing towards the tree line and then gone.

                    NASH (CONT'D)
          Hey!

Nash takes off in a sprint after the fleeing specter.

EXT.-NASH HOUSE-NIGHT

The figure disappears into the dark tree line, Nash racing fast across the lawn in close pursuit, bursting now, into...

EXT.-NASH HOUSE-FOREST-NIGHT

Nash continues running through the trees, slowing now, finally coming to a stop deep in the dark forest.  He looks around.  Moonlight.  Night bird CRIES.  But no sign of the mysterious figure.

(OVER) A RUSTLING.  Nash spins to his left, a shadow darting from tree to tree, there, then gone into the darkness.

                    NASH
          Hello?

(OVER) ANOTHER RUSTLING.  Nash spins to his right to glimpse another darting shadow, vanishing into the night.

                    NASH (CONT'D)
          Who's there?

That's when John is grabbed from behind.  His arms are pulled backwards in restraint as a figure steps out of the darkness.

Fedora and trench coat make him little more than an elegant shadow.  As he approaches, his face becomes visible in the moonlight.

                    NASH (CONT'D)
          Parcher.

(CONTINUED)

CONTINUED:

>                    PARCHER
>           It's good to see you, John.

Parcher nods and the man behind Nash releases him.  As the
stranger steps into the moonlight we see he is a U.S.
soldier.

>                    PARCHER (CONT'D)
>           What's wrong?  Cat got your tongue?

>                       NASH
>                     (finally)
>           You're not real.

Parcher wraps his arm around Nash.

>                    PARCHER
>           Don't be ridiculous.  Of course I am.
>           Let's take a walk.

He begins leading Nash deeper into the forest.

INT.-NASH HOUSE-NIGHT

Alicia lies in bed, her sleep fitful, moving under the covers. A
small MOAN escapes her lips, victim to dark dreams.

EXT.-FOREST-NIGHT

Parcher and his guard have led John to an old tool shed on
the edge of the property.

>                    PARCHER
>           The bomb is in its final position somewhere
>           in the continental U.S.

Parcher has walked to the front door.

>                    PARCHER (CONT'D)
>           Knowing your situation requires you keep a
>           low profile, Mohammed. We brought the
>           mountain to you.

Parcher pulls open the door, the night flooded with white light.
He bows and gestures with his arm, ushering Nash inside.

INT.-TOOL SHED-NIGHT

A mobile field unit. Portable lights hooked to a small
generator. Two or three more soldiers, working charts, sitting
in headphones over short wave radio consoles. Parcher leads Nash
to a lit map board.

(CONTINUED)

CONTINUED:

                    PARCHER
          We have narrowed the bomb's location to
          somewhere on the Eastern seaboard. But we
          can't pinpoint its exact position. Their
          codes have grown increasingly complex....

John stares at him.

                    PARCHER (CONT'D)
          What?

                    NASH
          You're hallucinations. Products of my
          imagination. Dr. Rosen said...

                    PARCHER
          Rosen? That quack? Schizophrenic break from
          reality, right? Psychological bullshit. Do
          I look imagined to you?

                    NASH
          Wheeler has no record of you....

                    PARCHER
          Do you think we list our personnel?

John just stares at him.

                    PARCHER (CONT'D)
          I'm sorry you had to go through this.
          Your actions must have looked bizarre to
          your wife. We had no idea she'd go ahead
          and have you institutionalized. But once
          she did....You were calling attention to
          yourself. I thought it best you stay put
          until the scrutiny passed.

                    NASH
          But Charles was at the hospital-

                    PARCHER
          After your lecture, we needed someone to
          keep an eye on you. Someone you would
          trust. Our operatives approached Charles.
          He's turned out to be quite good, actually.
          If only he didn't insist on carting that
          kid around everywhere.

Parcher nods and two figures step into the light. Charles, and
behind him, Marcee.

                    MARCEE
          Uncle John, Uncle John.

                                        (CONTINUED)

CONTINUED:


She races to him and leaps into his arms. He holds her so tight.

                    MARCEE (CONT'D)
          You're gonna squeeze me 'till I pop.

John reluctantly sets her down, his expression darkening. Turns
to Charles.

                    NASH
          At the hospital. Why couldn't Rosen see
          you?

                    PARCHER
          I can explain everything. But I need you to
          trust me.

HOLD on John a beat as he stares at William.

                    PARCHER (CONT'D)
          I've gone to great trouble to get you back.
          Make me owe you. I can restore your status
          at Wheeler. I can tell the world what you
          did, but...

Parcher walks right up to him, stares into his eyes.

                    PARCHER (CONT'D)
          I need you now, soldier. We all do.

John looks at Charles. At little Marcee. Finally...

                    NASH
          I was so scared you weren't real.

INT.-NASH HOUSE-LIVING ROOM-MORNING

John watches out the window as Alicia waves, drives off to work,
baby in the car with her.

                    PARCHER (OVER)
          Your wife cannot know anything this time.
          It's for her own protection.

EXT.-NASH HOUSE-DAY

Nash crosses the lawn, into the forest.

INT.-NASH HOUSE-TOOL SHED-NIGHT-MOS

Nash stands amidst the high tech machinery, before a light
board covered with maps and code, lecturing to a team of
analysts.

INT.-NASH HOUSE-FRONT HALL-AFTERNOON

Nash is carrying the baby upstairs as Alicia heads outside.

>                    ALICIA
>           There's a storm coming.

>                    NASH
>           I'll draw his bath.

Her concern flashes for only a second. But he registers it
anyway.

>                    NASH (CONT'D)
>           I'm his father, Alicia.
>                (softening)
>           It'll be ok.

Alicia's forced smile is full of hope. She heads outside.

EXT.-NASH HOUSE-AFTERNOON

Storm clouds assemble on the horizon. The wind is fierce. Alicia
gathers blanket and toys. (OVER) A distant BANGING from the
woods beyond the house.

Alicia looks up, puzzled. A beat. Then she leaves the detritus
on the lawn, begins heading towards the SOUND.

EXT.-FOREST-AFTERNOON

Alicia walks through the trees. In just minutes the sky has
grown darker. The wind has picked up, MOANING now.

(OVER) The BANGING has increased in both tempo and volume. She
heads towards...

EXT.-TOOL SHED-CONTINUOUS

The door to the old shed has been left ajar, BANGING in the
wind. Alicia approaches the shack. She pulls the door open.

INT.-TOOL SHED-CONTINUOUS

ALICIA-CLOSE. Face broken with horror as (OVER) RAIN begins to
PELT the roof. PULL BACK TO REVEAL...

The entire shed, walls, floor and ceiling are covered with
newspaper and magazine clippings, the hallmarks of John's
madness.

EXT.-LAWN-HIGH ANGLE-RAINING

See Alicia, tiny from this height, racing across the lawn towards the house. Lightening. (OVER) A THUD of distant thunder.

INT.-NASH HOUSE-RAINING

Alicia pushes inside. Looks in the living room. No sign of John. (OVER) From upstairs the sound of WATER RUNNING.

                    ALICIA
          No.

INT.-NASH HOUSE-STAIRWAY-CONTINUOUS

Alicia is racing up the stairs. (OVER) The sound of RUNNING WATER has grown LOUDER. Another lightening flash. A CRACK of thunder.

INT.-NASH BEDROOM-CONTINUOUS

Alicia bursts into the bedroom in time to see Nash struggling to close a window. The baby is nowhere in sight. (OVER) The sound of RUNNING WATER is loud from the bathroom.

                    NASH
               (back turned)
          I've almost got it. Charles, hold the baby
          up. Make sure he doesn't slip into the
          bath...

FOLLOW Alicia as she rushes into the room, past John's startled expression, and freezes in the open bathroom door.

INT.-NASH BATHROOM-CONTINUOUS

The baby is in the tub. Alone. The water is almost up to his chin, seconds from drowning. Alicia moves with lightning speed, grabbing her child up and into her arms.

                    ALICIA
          Precious baby, precious boy.

She clutches him for dear life. Spins to face John who's standing there, eyes wide with panic.

                    NASH
          Charles was watching him. He was okay.
          Charles was watching him.

                    ALICIA
               (hysterical)
          There's no one here!

                                        (CONTINUED)

CONTINUED:

                    NASH
          You don't understand. They've been
          injected with a cloaking serum. It's part
          of the war against the conspiracy...

Alicia holds his eyes. Then she's out the door. A beat. He
follows.

INT.-STAIRWAY-CONTINUOUS

Alicia is moving down the stairs, fast, baby in her arms. Nash
is chasing after her.

                    NASH
          I can see them because of a chemical that
          entered my bloodstream when my implant
          dissolved...

John follows her into...

INT.-LIVING ROOM-CONTINUOUS

                    NASH
          You couldn't know. It was for your own
          protection...

Alicia is already across the room, has begun dialing the phone,
tears of loss and rage spilling down her cheeks.

                    ALICIA
          Why can't you see that this doesn't make
          sense? Why can't you find one reason not to
          believe in them? To believe in us instead?
                    (into the phone)
          I need Doctor Rosen's office.

That's when Parcher steps into the doorway.

                    PARCHER
          You've got to stop her, John.

                    NASH
          Leave her out of this.

Alicia looks up to the doorway. No one there.

                    ALICIA
                    (blood draining)
          Who are you talking to?

                    NASH
          It wasn't her fault.

                                        (CONTINUED)

CONTINUED:

Parcher takes a step into the room.

                    PARCHER
          We can't afford to let her compromise us
          again.

                    ALICIA
          John, answer me, you're scaring me.

                    PARCHER
          You'll go back to the hospital.  Countless
          people will die.

                    NASH
          Alicia, please. Put the phone down.

                    PARCHER
          I can't let that happen.

Parcher opens his jacket, revealing a holster.

                    ALICIA
               (into the phone)
          Yes. Hello.

Parcher pulls his weapon. His eyes are sad.

                    PARCHER
          I'm sorry, John.

                    NASH
          No!

John rushes Parcher, knocking the gun from his hand, his body
simultaneously colliding with Alicia as he barrels past, sending
her into the wall.

                    NASH (CONT'D)
               (spinning)
          Alicia, I'm sorry-

                    PARCHER
          You know what to do, Nash.

                    NASH
               (spinning)
          Shut up!

                    ALICIA
               (almost a whisper)
          Get away from me.

(CONTINUED)

CONTINUED:

                    PARCHER
          Finish her.

                    NASH
          I wasn't trying to hurt you-

                    ALICIA
                 (screaming)
          GET AWAY!

John takes a step back from the force of her VOICE, and she's
pushing past him, out the door.

                    PARCHER
          She's too great a risk, John. You know
          what you have to do.

EXT.-NASH HOUSE-HIGH ANGLE-STORM-CONTINUOUS

Pouring rain. Alicia is making for their car, baby in her arms,
glancing over her shoulder.

INT.-NASH HOUSE-LIVING ROOM-CONTINUOUS

John stands staring at the door. Parcher steps forward, pointing
his now retrieved gun straight at John's head.

                    PARCHER
          It's her or you. Don't you get it?

Another figure comes down the steps. Charles.

                    CHARLES
          Oh God, John, do what he says.

A third tiny form tugs his hand. Marcee.

                    MARCEE
          Uncle John?

                    PARCHER
                 (cocking the hammer)
          Move, soldier. Now!

EXT.-NASH DRIVEWAY-STORM

Alicia is behind the wheel, the baby in the passenger seat, rain
beating on the windshield. She starts pulling away.

A figure runs out in front of the car, SLAMS both hands
against the hood. Stares at her through the glass.

                                        (CONTINUED)

CONTINUED:


                    NASH
          She never gets old.

His lips are shaking, rain spilling down his face like tears.

                    NASH (CONT'D)
          Marcee can't be real. She never gets old.

As Alicia emerges from the car, PULL BACK AND UP over two
small figures, staring at each other in the pouring rain.

EXT.-NASH HOUSE-DINING ROOM-LATE AFTERNOON

The rain has stopped. Nash and Alicia face a familiar figure
across the room. Dr. Rosen.

                    ROSEN
          Do you see them now?

                    NASH
          Yes.

REVERSE ANGLE. Marcee sits on the floor, playing Jacks.

                    ROSEN
          Why did you stop your meds, John?

SEE OVER Marcee to John as he turns, now, and looks at his wife.

                    NASH
          I couldn't work. I couldn't help with the
          baby. I couldn't touch you.
               (to Rosen)
          Is that better than being crazy?

                    ROSEN
          We need to start you on a higher run of
          insulin shocks. Then a new med-

                    NASH
          No. There has to be another way.

Charles is suddenly in the doorway, arms crossed.

                    NASH (CONT'D)
          There has to be another way.

Rosen stares at John a beat. Steeples his hands. Searching.

                    ROSEN
          John, your life is a kind of waking
          dream...


                                        (CONTINUED)

CONTINUED:


Rosen stops. Thinking. As Rosen resumes, Marcee walks to
Charles, and they EXIT.

                    ROSEN (CONT'D)
          When I dream, the dreaming world seems
          vivid, real. But as I wake, the richness of
          life, the very realness of experience
          elbows the dream from my mind....

                    NASH
          But what's in my head, to me, it's always
          been more real, most real...

                    ROSEN
               (nodding)
          Need a mathematical solution, your mind
          creates one. Lonely, your mind manufactures
          a best friend. Lack purpose, your mind
          creates a secret mission to save the world.

                    NASH
          Are you saying that is why I'm crazy or
          because I am crazy?

                    ROSEN
          Our current thinking varies-

John leans forward, predatory.

                    NASH
          You don't know, do you? You really don't
          know.

Rosen opens his hands.

                    ROSEN
          John, no one understands precisely what
          schizophrenia is. How it works-

                    NASH
          A problem.

John looks out at the window, turns back to Rosen.

                    NASH (CONT'D)
          A problem. That's all this is. A problem
          with no solution. That's what I do. Solve
          problems. It's what I am best at.

                    ROSEN
          John, this isn't a question of intellect-

                                        (CONTINUED)

                         NASH
              My dreams are more real than my life,
              isn't that what you said?

John turns to face Alicia.

                         NASH (CONT'D)
              So, I simply have to find a way to
              transpose those values-

                         ALICIA
                   (nodding)
              To make the experience of life more real
              than the dream-

                         NASH
              Then all this, the everyday, would
              displace the fantasies-

                         ALICIA
              And the delusions might fade, might
              ultimately disappear-

                         ROSEN
              Stop! Now! Both of you.

They turn to face him.

                         ROSEN (CONT'D)
              This isn't math. You can't come up with a
              formula to change the way you experience
              the world.

                         NASH
              I just have to apply my mind.

                         ROSEN
              There's no theorem. No proof. You can't
              reason your way out of this.

                         NASH
              Why not? Why can't I?

                         ROSEN
              Because your mind is where the problem is
              in the first place.

John opens his mouth. Closes it again. Takes a beat to re-group.

                         NASH
              I can work this out. I just need time...

CONTINUED:

>          ROSEN
> Schizophrenia is degenerative, John. Some
> days may be symptom free, but over time....
> You're getting worse.

(OVER) A tiny WHINE, like a distant cry. Nash looks up.

>          NASH
> Is that the baby?

>          ALICIA
> The baby's at my Mother's, John.

Nash looks up at Marcee, crossing the archway to the living
room. It is she who has begun to HUM.

>          ROSEN
> Without treatment, the fantasies may take
> over entirely.

INT.-NASH BEDROOM-LATE AFTERNOON

PAN ACROSS open drawers, a half packed suitcase, FIND Nash
sitting on the bed, holding Alicia's handkerchief, staring into
space.

>          ALICIA (OVER)
> Almost ready?

Alicia stands in the doorway, her expression brave.

>          ALICIA (CONT'D)
> Rosen's waiting outside.

Nash looks up to his wife, his smile sad enough to snap your
heart.

>          NASH
> I can't go back to the hospital.
>      (simple truth)
> I won't come home.

>          ALICIA
> He said if you said that.... He has
> commitment papers for me to sign.

Nash nods, so terribly tired. What he expected.

>          NASH
> Maybe you won't. Sign them, I mean. Maybe
> you'll give me some time. I'll try...maybe
> I can figure this out.

                                        (CONTINUED)

CONTINUED:


She steps towards him but he stops her with a gesture. Only as
he looks up do we really see the toll this is taking on him.

                    NASH (CONT'D)
          But whatever you do, I think Rosen's right
          about one thing. You shouldn't be here. I'm
          not safe anymore.

Alicia stands in the doorway. Staring at her husband.

                    ALICIA
          Would you have hurt me, John?

A figure races past behind her, Marcee, like a ghost,
startlingly fast, then gone. He looks up at his wife.

                    NASH
          ...I don't know.

Nash has to look away. When he looks back up, his wife is gone.
PUSH IN ON this single figure, sitting alone.

HOLD on John. (OVER) The SOUND of a car, PULLING AWAY. Nash
lowers his head, his expression a mask of loss and despair.

A SERIES OF CUTS. Nash sitting on the bed...WIDER on Nash,
still sitting, alone in the room...WIDER still THROUGH THE
WINDOW, Nash still sitting, so small, so alone.

NASH-CLOSE. John still hasn't moved, looks like he may never.

                    ALICIA (OVER)
          Rosen said to call if you try to kill me
          or anything.

THROUGH THE OPEN DOORWAY. Alicia stands in the bedroom,
looking at Nash, so picture perfect she can only be a
hallucination.

                    NASH
          You're still here.

                    ALICIA
          I'm still here.

She walks towards him now in the dying light.

                    ALICIA (CONT'D)
          You want to know what's real?

She kneels now, before him, takes his hand, puts it on her
cheek.


                                              (CONTINUED)

CONTINUED:

> ALICIA (CONT'D)
> This is real.

She stares into his eyes.

> ALICIA (CONT'D)
> This. Just this.

She reaches up and touches his face.

> ALICIA (CONT'D)
> What if the part of us that knows waking
> from the dream...
> (touches his head)
> What if it isn't here...
> (touches his heart)
> What if it's here?

She reaches up and touches his face with the soft back of her bent fingers, like half a prayer.

> ALICIA (CONT'D)
> I need to believe...that something
> extraordinary is possible.

And he moves into her arms, his tears finally coming now in RACKING SOBS, two small souls holding on to each other for dear life.

EXT.-PRINCETON UNIVERSITY-BLAIR STEPS-MORNING-FALL

Nash, in a baggy suit, climbs the steps. Students move across the common. The clothes may be different, but it's the same Princeton Nash entered so many years ago as a Freshman.

INT.-FINE HALL-HALLWAY-DAY

Nash stands before a door that reads CHAIR: MATH DEPARTMENT. Takes a step forward, a step back, repeats the tiny dance of indecision.

He pauses, pulls something out of his pocket. Alicia's rose embroidered handkerchief.

Holding it tight like a talisman, he KNOCKS on the door.

INT.-MATH DEPARTMENT-OFFICE

Helinger's office, once, years ago. A fellow sits, head bent over a desk, his face not yet visible to us. (OVER) A KNOCK.

> MAN (OVER)
> Come.

(CONTINUED)

CONTINUED:


Nash ENTERS, agitated, looking worn as he stands in the doorway.

                    NASH
          Hello, Martin.

The fellow looks up, familiar face going from confusion to
shock. It's Hansen.

                    HANSEN
          Jesus Christ.

                    NASH
          No. I don't have that one. My savior
          complex takes a different form.

Hansen just stares, his expression almost impossible to decode.

                    HANSEN
          I heard what happened. I wanted to write. I
          tried Macarthur but you had left and I
          just... God, how are you?

                    NASH
          Nutty as a fruitcake. And you?

Nash can't stay still, has moved now to a bookshelf displaying
an array of prizes, framed awards and medals.

                    NASH (CONT'D)
          You won after all.

                    HANSEN
          They were wrong, John. No one wins.

Nash just shakes his head tentative.

                    HANSEN (CONT'D)
          Sit down. Please.

Hansen returns to behind his desk.

                    HANSEN (CONT'D)
          I'm so glad to see you. What brings you
          back to Princeton?

                    CHARLES (OVER)
          Tell him you're a genius-

Nash spins over his shoulder to see Charles in the open doorway.

                    CHARLES (CONT'D)
          Tell him you're on a mission. Tell him your
          work is critical-

                                        (CONTINUED)

CONTINUED:


John gestures angrily for Charles to be quiet. Turns back to face Hansen, who stares a beat.

>                    NASH
>          Would you be willing to ignore what I just
>          did?

>                    HANSEN
>          What are old friends for?

>                    NASH
>          Is that what we are? Friends?

>                    HANSEN
>          Of course. We always have been.

A beat. Then John just shakes his head.

>                    NASH
>          Alicia and I think fitting in, being part
>          of community might do me good. That some
>          level of attachment to places, to other
>          people might help me sort of elbow out
>          these...
>               (looks up at the door)
>          Certain delusions that I have. It's only a
>          theory, how I might get better. It's a lot
>          to ask. And now that I'm here it occurs to
>          me you'll probably say no. But I was
>          wondering could I kind of hang around?

Hansen stares at him across the desk, this arch rival, this old friend. It is a long moment before he speaks. Then...

>                    HANSEN
>          Will you be needing an office?

EXT.-PRINCETON-CAMPUS PATH-DAY-WALKING

John walks the same path he traveled so many years ago. Students pour past him. John slows. Finally stops.

PULL BACK AND UP TO REVEAL...Nash stands alone, out of place amidst the ever-moving human sea.

INT.-FINE HALL-HALLWAY-AFTERNOON-WALKING

A young ADJUNCT is trailing Hansen down the stairs.

>                    ADJUNCT
>          So this guy tries to wander into the
>          library but he doesn't have ID...

                                        (CONTINUED)

CONTINUED:

>                    HANSEN
>     Why can't people read their memos...

>                    ADJUNCT
>     And he goes totally nuts...

They arrive at the picture window at the end of the hall. HANSEN
looks down, expression darkening...

THROUGH THE WINDOW-COURTYARD-HIGH ANGLE

Amidst a crowd of gaping students, Nash is storming the
courtyard in tight figure eights, CURSING at the empty air.

>                    HANSEN
>          Shit!

EXT.-PRINCETON COURTYARD-AFTERNOON

Nash walks his figure eights. Parcher keeps pace, matching
Nash step for step, right in his face.

>                    PARCHER
>     Is this what you are, Soldier? Some useless
>     ghoul. The local madman?

>                    NASH
>     I am not a soldier.

>                    PARCHER
>     You're going to end up old, in a cell.
>     Worthless. Discarded.

>                    NASH
>     There is no mission.

>                    PARCHER
>     And while you rock and drool, the world
>     will burn to ashes.

>                    NASH
>     You are not real.

>                    PARCHER
>     You're still talking to me.

Two campus cops peel away from the inside of the crowd, heading
towards Nash. Hansen gets there first, grabbing Nash.

>                    HANSEN
>          (shakes him)
>     John? John.

(CONTINUED)

CONTINUED:


Nash stops. Faces Hansen.

                    HANSEN (CONT'D)
          I'm sorry...

Nash is looking around. At the gaping students. The still wary
security guards. All staring at him.

                    HANSEN (CONT'D)
          I just heard what happened...

But John has stopped listening. His eyes are hollow with shame,
defeat. A beat. Then he walks off towards the gate.

                    HANSEN (CONT'D)
          Nash...

But John keeps walking. Parcher smiles. Opens his arm.

                    PARCHER
          Ladies and Gentleman, the great John
          Nash.

EXT.-NASH LAWN-EVENING

Alicia sits on the picnic table, the baby in his playpen on
the lawn before her. Nash stands over her, his shirt
untucked, tie half off. His face and posture are a portrait
of surrender.

                    NASH
          And their faces, the way they were all
          staring at me.

                    ALICIA
          John, stress can trigger the delusions-

                    NASH
          And then, on the way home, Charles was
          there again...

John looks away.

                    NASH (CONT'D)
          Sometimes I miss talking to him.

Alicia opens her mouth to speak. No words.

                    NASH (CONT'D)
          Maybe Rosen was right. Maybe I have to
          think about going to the hospital.


                                              (CONTINUED)

CONTINUED:

                           ALICIA
                        (searching)
            Maybe try again tomorrow.

(OVER) The baby WHIMPERS. John watches as Alicia goes to feed
him his binky. That's when Parcher steps INTO FRAME at John's
shoulder.

                        PARCHER
            The world peels back like an onion. Without
            us, Nash, what's left?

Nash just looks at Parcher, holds his eyes.

                    PARCHER (CONT'D)
            You see us. We see you. Who's to say
            what's real? What truth do you want?

John looks up, away from Parcher, fighting to ignore him.
Alicia comes up beside John, follows his gaze into the sky.

                        ALICIA
            Do you see the umbrella?

Nash looks over his shoulder a beat at Parcher, now standing
impossibly, a few feet away.

                        NASH
            No. Just stars.

Parcher shakes his head, turns and walks away.

                        ALICIA
            Here. Let me show you.

As Alicia slides her arm around John, HOLD on this couple,
standing together against all the dark in the world.

EXT.-NASH HOUSE-MORNING

Alicia stands facing Nash in the doorway, kisses him softly.
With the expression of a man going to war, he sets off down the
path.

Charles and Marcee fall in, trailing silently behind.

INT.-FINE HALL-MORNING

Students file into a classroom. Nash faces Charles and Marcee,
Alicia's handkerchief in his hand for courage.

                        CHARLES
            You can't ignore me forever.

                                       (CONTINUED)

CONTINUED:

                    NASH
          You were a good friend to me. The best. But
          I won't talk to you again.

Nash bends on one knee before Marcee. He barely touches her
cheek before she begins to cry, tiny breathless SOBS.

                    NASH (CONT'D)
          Or you either, baby girl.
               (kisses her head)
          Goodbye.

A PROFESSOR comes to the doorway, stops to stare at this odd man
on his knee, kissing thin air. Nash rises, faces the Professor.

                    NASH (CONT'D)
          I was wondering if I might audit your
          seminar?

The young Professor's eyes narrow. He seems suddenly
flustered.

                    PROFESSOR
          Oh. Of course. Dr. Hansen mentioned-
          It's...it's an honor sir.

John is about to step through the door. He stops. Over his
shoulder a figure stands watching down the hall. Parcher.

                    PROFESSOR (CONT'D)
          Is something wrong?

                    NASH
          It's my first class.

Nash steps over the threshold.

INT.-PRINCETON-LIBRARY-DAY

TRACK PAST a librarian, PAST oak tables and green reading
lights to FIND Nash, scrawling symbols over a window with a
wax pencil, pacing, MUMBLING to himself.

Nash stops, rests his head against the glass, defeated,
looking down at the campus below. What he sees is startling.
See it now...

EXT-PRINCETON COURTYARD-SPRING-DAY

Nash walks in figure eights, silent as Parcher SHOUTS at him.

Students pass without a second glance, folks used to him.
Nash looks past Parcher to see...

EXT.-PRINCETON HENRY QUAD ARCHES-FALL-DAY-1963

A figure walks towards the gate. CAMERA TURNS TO REVEAL a
slightly older Nash. He is met by a slightly older Alicia.
Nash looks disheveled, beaten by the day. Alicia smoothes his
hair, adjusts his tie.  Nash glances up...

EXT.-PRINCETON CAMPUS-SUMMER-DAY

Nash is crossing campus, head down, briefcase clutched in his
hugging arms.

WIDER. Three students trail, heads down, books hugged to
their chests in taunting mimicry. Nash looks up to see...

EXT.-PRINCETON COMMON-BLAIR STEPS-SPRING-DAY

Nash climbs the familiar steps. Around him, at least half the
passing students are female. Through the crowd, he catches a
glimpse of a familiar figure staring at him, eyes wide. Marcee.
Nash looks over his shoulder to see...

EXT.-PRINCETON COURTYARD-SPRING-DAY

Nash rides his bicycle in figure eights. PULL UP TO REVEAL...

EXT.-PRINCETON LIBRARY WINDOW-FALL-DAY-1978

A figure looks down at campus through rows of symbols that cover
the glass before him. It's Nash, twelve years older than when we
left him here.

INT.-LIBRARY-FALL-MINUTES LATER

Nash turns away from the window, goes back to his pad on one of
the oak reading tables.

> VOICE (OVER)
> Did you just solve Riemann?

John looks up to face a SKINNY student who gestures to the large
circular window, covered now with orderly rows of symbols.

> NASH
> This analogue to Frobenius only works for a
> sporadic family of noncommutative
> extensions. So, no. But I'm making
> progress.

> STUDENT
> You're John Nash, right?

The Student PLONKS his textbook on the table. Opens it.

(CONTINUED)

CONTINUED:

      STUDENT (CONT'D)
  I've been studying your equilibrium.

TEXT BOOK-CLOSE. Under the title FUNDAMENTALS IN MATHEMATICS is
Nash's Equilibrium. Nash smiles, this is news.

      STUDENT (CONT'D)
  To come up with something totally original
  the way you did...

The kid slides his notebook towards Nash.

      STUDENT (CONT'D)
  I've been developing a theory. I believe I
  can show that Galois extensions are
  covering spaces. That everything is
  connected. That it's all one subject. Maybe
  you could take a look.

John looks at this boy, the fevered ambition in his eyes so
bright, so familiar. A beat. Nash shuts the boy's notebook.

      NASH
  When was the last time you ate?

The boy stares at him blankly. Nash reaches into his lunch bag.

      NASH (CONT'D)
  You know, food?

Nash slides half a sandwich across to the puzzled boy.

      NASH (CONT'D)
  The woman loves mayonnaise.

EXT.-PRINCETON-MAIN GATE-AFTERNOON

Alicia, now ten years older, gentle lines around her eyes,
stands waiting. Checks her watch. Nervous. Hansen walks up.

      HANSEN
  Hurry. You need to see something.

INT.-PRINCETON LIBRARY-DAY-MOMENTS LATER

Alicia stands just behind Hansen, her eyes wide.

      ALICIA
  Oh.

Nash sits with the Skinny student, talking intently about a
series of equations written on a free standing blackboard.

           (CONTINUED)

CONTINUED:

                    NASH
          ...And the bicycle travels continuously at
          a rate of twenty miles per hour and the fly
          travels back and forth from tire to tire so
          how far is the fly from it's starting point
          in one hour?

The student glances up at him, anxious. Nash smiles.

                    NASH (CONT'D)
          I said the bike is going twenty miles an
          hour. So that's how far the fly goes.
          Twenty miles. That's the point. Listen.

The way Nash explains, the way the kid reacts, how they both
LAUGH, they look like nothing more than professor and student.

HOLD on Alicia, eyes sparkling. And she smiles.

EXT.-PRINCETON-FALL-DAY-WALKING

Long-haired students toss frisbees, play hacky-sack. Nash and
Hansen walk together. No words. Finally...

                    NASH
          I was thinking I might teach.

                    HANSEN
          A classroom with fifty students is daunting
          for anyone. And you're a terrible teacher,
          John.

                    NASH
          Details, details.

                    HANSEN
          What about, you know... Are they gone?

                    NASH
          Oh no, they're not gone. Maybe they will
          never be.

Nash looks back over his shoulder. Walking behind them are
Charles, William and Marcee. They stare at him with little
emotion.

                    NASH (CONT'D)
          But I've gotten used to ignoring them. And
          I think, as a result, they've kind of given
          up on me. Do you think that's the way it is
          with our dreams and our nightmares? That we
          have to keep feeding them for them to stay
          alive?

                                        (CONTINUED)

CONTINUED:

                    HANSEN
          But they haunt you?

                    NASH
          They're my past, Martin. Everybody is
          haunted by their past. Do you understand?

                    HANSEN
          Maybe. Almost.

They have come, now, to one of the stone gaming tables where a
couple of kids are finishing up a game of GO, stones CLICKING.

                    NASH
          I've got to go. Alicia still worries if I'm
          late. You get a lot of attention when
          you're crazy.

                    HANSEN
          I'll talk to the department. Maybe in the
          Spring.

John nods, begins to head off.

                    HANSEN (CONT'D)
          Hey, Nash.

Nash spins. Hansen TAPS the game board in front of him. Flips a
stone and catches it in his hand.

                    HANSEN (CONT'D)
          You scared?

John stares at him. Then he grins.

As John goes and sits down, PULL BACK AND UP over these two old
friends, playing with the hearts of the boys they once were.

INT.-PRINCETON-FINE HALL-1990'S

THE DOOR swings open. Nash emerges amidst a gaggle of students.
The way the students cling to him, JABBERING, this man is one
fine teacher.

                    MAN (OVER)
          Professor Nash?

A MAN is standing by the doorway. This is THOMAS KING. Nash's
smile is polite, but vaguely puzzled. Turns to a female STUDENT.

                    NASH
          Do you see him?

                                              (CONTINUED)

CONTINUED:


The girl shrugs, nods.

                    NASH (CONT'D)
          You'll forgive me. I'm always suspicious of
          new people.

Although King is puzzled, the students seem to take it in
stride. They just like this guy.

                    STUDENT
          See you next week, Professor.

Nash watches them go, smiling, paternal.

                    NASH
          I have a son that age. Harvard.
               (rolls his eyes)
          So, now that you are real, who are you and
          what can I do you for?

King takes a beat before speaking. Then...

                    KING
          Professor, my name is Thomas King. I am
          here to tell you you are being considered
          for the Nobel Prize.

EXT.-PRINCETON HOLDER ARCHES-SPRING-WALKING

Nash and King walk. Students who pass greet Nash.

                    NASH
          I'm sorry. I'm just a bit stunned.

                    KING
          Over the last ten years your work in game
          theory has become a foundation of modern
          economics.

                    NASH
          Suddenly everybody likes that one. What
          about my work on manifold embedding-

                    KING
          Your equilibrium's applications to FCC
          bandwidth auctions, to anti-trust cases-

                    NASH
          Anti-trust cases? Huh? I never would have
          thought of that.

They walk through a familiar doorway...

INT.-FACULTY LOUNGE-CLOAK ROOM

No white-jacketed valets. In the main room, High Tea is in progress. The formal dress is gone. The students are multi-national, some waiters women. But the ritual is the same.

                KING
      Shall we have some tea?

Nash stares through the archway a long beat. When he looks back at King, his eyes are sad.

                NASH
      I don't really go in there.

There is a tragic tenderness to his expression, an acknowledgement of all that has been lost to time.

             NASH (CONT'D)
      I usually just take a sandwich in the
      library.

King puts his hand on the small of John's back. John slips something out of his pocket. Alicia's handkerchief, rubbing it gently before, finally, he steps over the threshold.

INT.-FACULTY LOUNGE-MOMENTS LATER

Nash and King sit across from each other. A young girl serves them tea from a silver service. Nash smiles at her.

                NASH
      Things have changed.

The sentence seems to resonate more deeply to him than he had intended. He grows pensive a beat. Then...

             NASH (CONT'D)
      I thought the nominations for the Nobel
      Prize were secret. I thought you only knew
      if you won or lost.

                KING
      That is generally the case, yes. But these
      are special circumstances. The awards are
      substantial. They require private funding.
      As such, the image of the Nobel is quite
      important...

King stops a beat. Takes a sip of tea.

                                    (CONTINUED)

CONTINUED:

                    NASH
          So you came here to see if I was crazy. To
          see if I'd screw everything up if I
          actually won. Maybe dance at the podium or
          strip naked and squawk like a chicken.

It's Nash's tone that puts King at ease.

                    KING
          Something like that, yes.

Nash stops, stares off. Then...

                    NASH
          Would I embarrass you? Yes, I suppose it's
          possible. You see, I am crazy. I take the
          newer medications. I still see things that
          are not here. But I choose to ignore them.
          Like a diet of the mind. I do not indulge
          certain appetites. My appetite for
          patterns. And perhaps my appetite to
          imagine, even to dream. I have lost much.
          But...

He opens his hands.

                    YOUNG PROFESSOR
          Professor Nash?

John looks up. A young faculty member is staring at him. He
reaches into his pocket, lays something down in front of him.
It's his pen.

WIDER

Another teacher stands behind him. He too lays his pen down
before Nash. And now everyone in the room is rising, coming
to him, laying their pens down, one after another in a
growing tribute to a lifetime of accomplishment.

                    KING
          What...?

The pens keep coming. Nash opens his mouth to answer. But he
can't, eyes suddenly flooding with tears for this journey taken
so very far.

                                        DISSOLVE TO:

INT.-ROYAL SWEDISH ACADEMY-NOBEL CEREMONY

A giant hall. Full. Nash stands at the podium, blinking his
eyes. Hundreds sit watching, as camera flashbulbs finally cease.

                                        (CONTINUED)

CONTINUED:


But Nash just stands there. A long beat. And even longer.

KING-CLOSE. In the audience. Concerned.

ALICIA-CLOSE. In the front row. Starting to worry.

BACK TO NASH. Still standing there. See what he sees. Hundreds
of faces staring back at him. Finally, just when all seems
lost...

> NASH
> Thank you. Thank you for your patience.

But he's not looking at the speech before him. He's not looking
at the audience. He's looking only at Alicia.

> NASH (CONT'D)
> I have always believed in numbers. In the
> equations and logics that lead to reason. I
> was wrong. It is only in the mysterious
> equations of love that any logic or reason
> can be found. Perhaps it is good to have a
> beautiful mind. But a better gift is to
> discover a beautiful heart.

*And suddenly there is no one else in the room but the two of
them, Nash's magical vision revealing the patterns of the heart.*

> NASH (CONT'D)
> Thank you for your belief in me after so
> many years. You are the reason I am here
> today.

Nash reaches into his breast pocket and takes out something
familiar. It's her rose embroidered handkerchief.

> NASH (CONT'D)
> You are the reason I am.

And with that he tucks the handkerchief in his suit pocket.

> NASH (CONT'D)
> Thank you.

The room EXPLODES with APPLAUSE, suddenly full again. Hansen
stands, his APPLAUSE ever more enthusiastic, as does Sol, and
Bender, and then those around them, all rising in ovation.

ALICIA-CLOSE. CLAPS as hard as the rest, full of love and pride.

John just stands on stage. Taking it all in. Then, finally, he
bows, folks APPLAUDING so loud that Nash can't stifle a LAUGH.

INT.-ROYAL SWEDISH ACADEMY-COCKTAIL RECEPTION

John stands with Alicia and amidst the dwindling well
wishers.

> ALICIA
> Time to go?

> NASH
> Yes, please.

He helps her on with her wrap.  That's when he sees them,
standing by the door.  Three familiar figures.  Charles,
Marcee and William.

Then Parcher does something odd. He gives Nash a small salute.

> ALICIA
> What is it? What's wrong?

He turns to his wife. His smile is long in coming, but when it
comes, it melts the worry on his face along with our hearts.

> NASH
> Nothing. Nothing at all.

He takes her hand, turning his back on them, man and wife
heading away together, outside, into the light and gone.

> FINAL FADE TO BLACK.

# STILLS

RUSSELL CROWE
as mathematical genius John Forbes Nash, Jr.

PAUL BETTANY
as Nash's Princeton roommate Charles Hermann

JENNIFER CONNELLY
as Nash's wife Alicia, a brilliant MIT physics student

ED HARRIS
as government agent William Parcher

CHRISTOPHER PLUMMER
as the mysterious Dr. Rosen

Nash (RUSSELL CROWE) during his days as a graduate student at Princeton.

Rivals Nash (RUSSELL CROWE) and Hansen (JOSH LUCAS) engage in a game of Go, a popular past-time during their graduate school days at Princeton.

Nash (RUSSELL CROWE) proposes marriage to Alicia (JENNIFER CONNELLY).

Nash (RUSSELL CROWE) is caught up in pursuit of a truly original idea.

Nash (RUSSELL CROWE) is exhausted by the top-secret work he does for Parcher (ED HARRIS).

Nash (RUSSELL CROWE) delivers a guest lecture at Harvard.

Screenwriter AKIVA GOLDSMAN and director RON HOWARD

AKIVA GOLDSMAN, RUSSELL CROWE, and RON HOWARD reviewing a scene.

RON HOWARD, RUSSELL CROWE, BRIAN GRAZER, and AKIVA GOLDSMAN on the set.

# PRODUCTION NOTES

*A Beautiful Mind* is inspired by events in the life of John Forbes Nash, Jr., and in part based on the biography *A Beautiful Mind* by Sylvia Nasar. Born to a middle class family in a small West Virginia town on June 13, 1928, Forbes has been a figure of fascination in the world of ideas for more than 50 years. His pioneering work in the field of game theory made him the star of the "new mathematics" in the 1950s, but he disappeared from the scene during the long years that schizophrenia distorted his life. Nevertheless, game theory became a vital element of business and economics during his absence. By 1994, Nash had regained control of his life and was again active as a scholar. That year, he received the Nobel Prize in Economic Science, along with John C. Harsanyi and Richard Selten, "for their pioneering analysis of equilibria in the theory of non-cooperative games." (Non-cooperative games are those in which no outside authority enforces a set of predetermined rules.)

*A Beautiful Mind* began its way to the screen when producer Brian Grazer read a *Vanity Fair* article about John Forbes Nash, Jr. Grazer was fascinated by writer Sylvia Nasar's true story of the mathematical genius who won international acclaim, then lost it all to schizophrenia. What made the story truly exceptional was the fact that Nash eventually recovered enough to return to work and later win the Nobel Prize.

"I loved this story because it was about survival," said Grazer. "And I also loved that it was about genius as expressed through the root of competitiveness." After seeing early galleys of Nasar's biography on Nash, Grazer engaged in some competition himself to obtain the film rights to her book. "I saw that the story could present a visceral experience for an audience," Grazer said.

Grazer hired Akiva Goldsman to write the screenplay. Goldsman brought an immensely singular perspective to the project. His parents, therapist Tev Goldsman and renowned child psychologist Mira Rothenberg, had founded one of America's first "group homes" for emotionally disturbed children in the family's Brooklyn residence. Akiva Goldsman grew up side by side with children who occupied their own delusional worlds. His unique understanding of the material and his desire to explore the dramatic line between reality and delusion made him the only choice for Grazer.

Goldsman took on the assignment with strong ideas on how to structure the narrative. "It's not a literal telling of Nash's life," the writer explained. "I tried to take the architecture of his life—his genius, his schizophrenia, his Nobel Prize—and from that constructed a semi-fictional story." Goldsman received a "written by" rather than "screenplay by" credit for *A Beautiful Mind* from the Writers Guild of America, which signals extraordinary innovation and a distinctive departure from the source material.

Although many directors wanted the project, Grazer and his Imagine partner Ron Howard quickly found that they were in complete harmony on how to best approach the adaptation. "Ron has succeeded at the challenges of every genre," said Grazer, "and has demonstrated particular strength in creating three-dimensional characters, which is critically important with this film."

The two partners had spent years looking for a project that dealt with mental illness and its impact on people and their families. "When you read about it, you realize that mental illness is so prevalent," Howard said. "People didn't always have the right terms for it, but most families have had a brush with it. The story of John Nash is an amazing, powerful journey. But as unique as this man is, his story is also very accessible because it is so heartbreakingly human."

Grazer and Howard were also drawn to the love story at the heart of *A Beautiful Mind*. "John Nash's victory wasn't only that he beat schizophrenia or that he won the Nobel Prize," said Grazer. "The victory in the movie and in his life is how the love between him and Alicia survived and grew and evolved."

"It's a grown-up kind of romance," Howard added. "The relationship was intensely complex, as were the challenges that Alicia and John faced together.

"John Nash's journey is incredibly heroic, but so is Alicia's," Howard continued. "Alicia is very interesting—she's kind of the belle of the ball, you know? Gorgeous, intelligent, and very, very interested in John Nash. And what she bargains for is not what she gets. It winds up being an incredible challenge for her as a human being."

Nasar, the author of the Nash biography, was inspired by Alicia's strength. "Nash never would have survived without Alicia," she said. "To me, she was the heroine of the book, and she's the heroine of the movie."

Nasar was pleased that the project landed in the hands of Grazer and

Howard. "I did not have the expectation that it was going to be a documentary," she emphasized. "Nash's story is like a fairy tale, in that it can be told many different ways, because it's so rich and has so much emotional power. The screenplay captures the essence of the story."

## CASTING FOR GENIUS ...

*A Beautiful Mind* brings together a unique ensemble of actors—major stars, distinguished veterans, exciting newcomers—who create intense chemistry. "There's an element of danger with a number of these actors—especially Russell Crowe, Ed Harris, and Christopher Plummer," said Howard. "They project an unpredictability and volatility that might surprise people in a movie perceived as human interest or intellectual. There's always a palpable, visceral tension with them onscreen, the threat of some kind of explosion."

Grazer and Howard cast the Academy Award®-winning Crowe in the role of John Nash well before the actor's immense success with *Gladiator*. "I zeroed in on Russell because he can communicate so intensely without words," explained Grazer, who had been especially taken with Crowe in *L.A. Confidential* and *The Insider*. "And that's what you need to do with John Nash."

Howard was also a fan. "We're telling the story of someone who was viewed as an Adonis in his field," said the director. "Russell's physicality and charisma were a real asset, as were his intellect, his mental toughness and his soulfulness. It's a rare blend—and so important for the story of Nash. Brian and I both really wanted the movie to have some edge and *not* be a sentimentalized look at this man's life. Russell wanted that, too."

Crowe was drawn to the project for a number of reasons. He had an immediate and strong reaction to the screenplay. "There are a couple of cinematic tricks built into the script which are very special," he said. "Akiva Goldsman did an incredibly smart job of identifying the salient points of John Nash's story that would make for a compelling feature film."

Crowe also appreciated the opportunity to put a human face on schizophrenia. "To simply illustrate that a schizophrenic is the same as anybody who has any kind of sickness was important," he said. "Their lives are still 'normal,' in that they still fall in love, have babies, want to achieve things."

The project also marked a personal achievement for Crowe, who had long wanted to work with Howard and Grazer. "Ron's pedigree as a filmmaker is impeccable," Crowe said. "He and Brian work really well together, and their body of work as a production team is very impressive."

Grazer and Howard's productions include the 1997 film *Inventing the Abbotts*, which starred Jennifer Connelly in a performance that both partners admired. Since then, Connelly has distinguished herself in such films as *Requiem for a Dream* and *Pollock*.

Howard quickly knew that he wanted Connelly in this film. "Jennifer has really emerged in the last few years. She's very intelligent, a great beauty, and has a lot of integrity. And she's developing this extraordinary screen presence," he said. "She had a clear understanding of what made this movie so compelling and involving."

She also had strong chemistry with Crowe. "We had many actresses read with Russell," Grazer said. "When you do those private readings, you can immediately sense if there is chemistry. You want to know if the actress can challenge him in a way that will keep him at the top of his game. Jennifer more than held her own."

The filmmakers cast Ed Harris as William Parcher, Nash's boss at the Department of Defense. Their previous collaboration with Harris in *Apollo 13* had led to an Academy Award® nomination for the actor. Howard felt that Harris embodied a mysterious quality that was essential for this film. "William Parcher is a government agent who recruits John Nash into a kind of secret world, and it ends up being more complicated and dangerous than Nash had ever expected," said Howard. "Ed Harris is a little elusive; you can't always be sure what his agenda might be. He's also a really powerful actor who can go toe to toe with Russell."

As for toe to toe, the night before principal photography on *A Beautiful Mind* began, Crowe and Harris were at the Academy Awards® ceremony. Both had been nominated in the Best Actor category, Crowe for *Gladiator* and Harris for *Pollock*, a film he also directed. "It was possibly not the best way to start a relationship," joked Crowe, who won the award. "But Ed is an absolute gentleman."

Crowe and Harris weren't the only company members who attended the Oscars® on the eve of production. Cinematographer Roger Deakins had been nominated for *O Brother, Where Art Thou?* and costume designer Rita Ryack was a nominee for *Dr. Seuss' How The Grinch Stole Christmas*.

## THE PRINCETON CREW ... and the Mysterious Dr. Rosen ...

*A Beautiful Mind* begins with Nash's arrival at Princeton University, which had become the top school for the advanced study of mathematics a few years earlier. Though socially awkward, Nash eventually befriends fellow math students Sol and Bender, who go on to work with him at MIT's Wheeler Lab.

For the role of Sol, the filmmakers cast Adam Goldberg, who had co-starred in *Saving Private Ryan* and in their own *Ed TV*. Anthony Rapp, who starred in *Rent* on Broadway, was cast as Bender. "We're Nash's compatriots," Rapp said of the duo. "We rag on him for being so eccentric, but we're the guys who follow him through his life."

Nash's Princeton roommate Charles actually encourages his eccentricities. British actor Paul Bettany, who played Chaucer in *A Knight's Tale*, relished that role. "Charles reflects the chaotic bit of John," said Bettany, "and allows him to do things like throw desks through windows."

A Princeton student named Hansen engages in an intense rivalry with Nash. "They are both completely filled with their own sense of destiny," said Josh Lucas, who played Hansen and previously co-starred in *You Can Count on Me*. "Hansen is obviously well-bred and has the silver spoon, but he is deeply threatened by Nash."

Oscar® nominee Judd Hirsch (*Ordinary People*) plays Nash's Princeton advisor, Professor Helinger. "We didn't want a soul-less bureaucrat in this role," Howard emphasized. "We needed someone with personal charisma who could hold the screen with Russell. Judd is just right because he projects intellect with humanity, and he can hold his own with anybody in anything."

*A Beautiful Mind* reunites Russell Crowe with Christopher Plummer, the acclaimed actor who portrays Dr. Rosen. "Russell is one of the most versatile actors on the screen today," said Plummer, a stage and screen veteran who starred opposite Crowe in *The Insider*. "Here, he goes back to disguising himself in a role which is obviously going to be huge for him. He is the right kind of person for a demanding role like this, because he will not let one detail go by."

Despite the numerous films each has made, Howard and Plummer had never met before *A Beautiful Mind*. "Dr. Rosen comes into Nash's life at a time when Nash can't be sure whom to trust," Howard reflected. "So it was really important to have an actor who offered some true complexity in his choices. Christopher Plummer is one of those great actors who knows how to find the subtlety and subtext in a character and in a scene."

Plummer understood the challenge. "It's an interesting role, because he starts out a little edgy, and the audience should not really know who or what he is," the actor explained. "I was enchanted by the script, not just because it was well-written and well-constructed, but because it was so unbelievably touching, and heart wrenching, and very tough and unsentimental."

Plummer also appreciated Howard's working style. "He's like the old-fashioned director who trusts his company. I think the best directors are the ones who know how to cast. And once they've cast, they almost leave you alone because they've got the family, and they trust the family."

## GETTING IT RIGHT ...

The filmmakers treated every step of the production of *A Beautiful Mind* with respect. "There is a lot of creativity in the story-telling and we've taken license to try to condense a lifetime into a film, but we are presenting a real world," said Howard. "We approached this story as truthfully as possible and tried to let authenticity be our guide."

To heighten the feeling of realism and maximize the emotional truth of *A Beautiful Mind*, the filmmakers decided to shoot the story in continuity. Filming a movie's scenes in the actual order of the story is an extremely rare practice and a true luxury in filmmaking today. Though logistically difficult, it is immensely helpful to actors, and it was Crowe who initially suggested it for *A Beautiful Mind*. Howard had worked this way as an actor in George Lucas's *American Graffitti*, and he shot the scenes within his three major locations in *Apollo 13* in order, so he was aware of the benefits.

"This movie is really a performance piece and very emotionally challenging," Howard reflected. "We took a life's journey in our three months of filming. Russell's journey as John Nash is complex and emotional with profound psychological shifts from scene to scene—plus he ages more than 40 years. The effectiveness of working this way comes from the connectedness the actors feel with what they're going through. The work takes a more natural course. All the actors were thrilled."

It was also beneficial to Howard and director of photography Roger Deakins. "The film shifts stylistically from era to era, and from phase to phase of Nash's life," Howard explained. "The tone, lighting, and composition shifted with Nash's psychological and emotional states, his level of duress, and the emotional connection he felt or didn't feel with Alicia, his colleagues, or his own ideas.

"By shooting in order, Roger and I could be more exacting and fluid in how we made our choices. We had the opportunity to be inspired by what we saw the actors doing and what we learned about the story as we filmed it."

Before beginning principal photography on March 27, 2001, in Princeton, New Jersey, Howard scheduled two weeks of rehearsal with the actors. "We put the scenes on their feet to see how they played," said screenwriter Goldsman.

During pre-production, Howard and executive producer Todd Hallowell invited John Nash himself to lecture them on his work, with the idea of studying the mathematician's style at a blackboard and of gaining even a slight understanding of his work. "The real benefit was that we saw Nash really being Nash, and operating on his terms in his world," said Howard.

"*A Beautiful Mind* is not some kind of math lesson," he added, "but we did a tremendous amount of research to try to get it right. We've been as diligent as we were with the mission control and flight depictions in *Apollo 13*." Barnard College mathematics professor Dave Bayer was on set every day as the company's math watchdog and took the actors involved in the Princeton sequences to meet his fellow mathematicians.

A careful researcher of his roles, Crowe had to be resourceful to create the character of John Nash—not just for one chapter of his life, but for a turbulent 47-year span. "The difficult thing is that even though Nash was famous in mathematics circles, he was not at all a public figure," Crowe said. "He wasn't really documented, so I didn't have any footage of him as a young man."

Crowe watched recent videotapes of the mathematician, read Sylvia Nasar's biography *A Beautiful Mind*, and studied Nash's writings. He also studied documentaries about schizophrenia. In addition, Crowe tried to find out how the mind of a mathematical genius actually works. "Nash's mind is much more the way we think of an artist's mind, rather than a scientist's mind," he observed. "He can look at a series of equations and simply know the answer."

Because of their schedules, Crowe and Nash were unable to meet prior to filming, but Nash, who lives in Princeton, did visit the set during location filming at Princeton early in the shoot. "I met him that day and got some very valuable things from just standing in front of him," recalled Crowe, who invited Nash to have tea while watching filming. Nash visited again with Alicia and their son Johnny when the production returned to Princeton in June.

Connelly was grateful to meet with Alicia Nash. "It was wonderful to be able to run things by her and ask her to share memories," Connelly said. "When I asked if there was anything she wanted to express to me, that she'd really like to see in the film, she as much as said, 'It's yours.'"

The other actors all found their own ways into character. In addition to the expected research of watching films from the 1940s and 1950s and reading books about the post-World War II period, some learned to play "Go," the complicated, 3000-year-old board game that sparks a competition among the Princeton students in *A Beautiful Mind*.

## THE LOOK...

While doing his own extensive research for *A Beautiful Mind*, production designer Wynn Thomas found that the Princeton campus, where the company filmed for just over two weeks, has not changed much in the past 50 years. "Ron referred to Nash's time at Princeton as the *Life Magazine* portion of the picture," Thomas said. "And it still has that idyllic feel."

Costume designer Rita Ryack had access to photographic archives and people who knew John Nash for her Princeton research. Crowe's wardrobe included pieces that Nash had worn, such as his Converse All-Star sneakers, which were definitely not the norm at Princeton back then.

The other universities depicted in *A Beautiful Mind*, MIT and Harvard, were actually filmed at schools in New York. "Bronx Community College has a series of classical revival buildings designed by Stanford White, which are not unlike the buildings at MIT," said production designer Thomas. The brick, colonial-style architecture of Manhattan College in the Bronx filled in for Harvard.

After the early Princeton years, Nash teaches at MIT and works at Wheeler Lab, a think-tank where top academics worked for the military during the Cold War era. Thomas created the film's Wheeler Lab in an abandoned wing of the imposing Garden State Cancer Center, a research facility in Belleville, New Jersey. A spectacular Pentagon war room, with walls of numbers that Nash is asked to decode, was built in a basement at Fordham University in the Bronx. The huge 1950s computers in that scene were created by Thomas's team.

William Parcher's secret command center, filled with futuristic technical equipment, greatly impresses Nash in the film. Parcher's computers, very advanced for the period in which the scene takes place, are based on 1960s models.

Built on a stage at the Military Ocean Terminal in Bayonne, New Jersey, the command center and office is an imposing, self-contained world with curved walls. "I chose to design sets that did not have straight walls because Nash's point of view of those worlds is so off-kilter," Thomas explained.

The scene in which Nash and Alicia attend a ball at the Massachusetts Governor's mansion was filmed at Fairleigh Dickinson University in New

Jersey, and featured hundreds of extras in vintage ball gowns with full skirts and crinolines. In contrast, Alicia wears a chic black gown, with a red bow in back. "She had a nice slim silhouette, where all the women around her looked like cupcakes," said costume designer Ryack. "We wanted her to look like she was surrounded by magic."

The couple's wedding scene, in which Connelly wears a vintage dress from Priscilla of Boston, was filmed at St. Mark's Church in Manhattan's East Village. Not long after their marriage, John Nash finds himself in Dr. Rosen's office, a sumptuous space dominated by a painting that hung in Freud's home. "When Nash wakes up in this space, he's supposed to be disoriented, as is the audience," said Thomas. "We're trying to take the audience on the same journey that Nash is on."

That standard was applied throughout the film. Special effects, for example, show how Nash's mind sorts numbers in solving mathematical problems. Telling the story from Nash's point of view, the filmmakers felt, would make mental illness more understandable.

"*A Beautiful Mind* encompasses a lot of powerful, dramatic territory," said Howard. "It deals with genius, madness, love, fear and creativity. It's a very humanistic telling of the story, very accessible. It's a labor of love."

It's also a movie where people enjoyed themselves on the set. While in make-up as the 70-year-old Nash, Crowe enjoyed walking the streets of downtown Princeton totally unrecognized. Greg Cannom, who also created his make-up for *The Insider*, did such realistic work that when filming the Nobel Prize scene, a costumer mistook Crowe for one of the many white-tie-attired seniors in the auditorium.

Filming of *A Beautiful Mind* wrapped on June 28, 2001, in Bayonne, New Jersey.

UNIVERSAL PICTURES   DREAMWORKS PICTURES   IMAGINE ENTERTAINMENT Present

# A BEAUTIFUL MIND

Directed by RON HOWARD    Written by AKIVA GOLDSMAN
Produced by BRIAN GRAZER And RON HOWARD
Executive Producers KAREN KEHELA    TODD HALLOWELL

RUSSELL CROWE    ED HARRIS    JENNIFER CONNELLY    PAUL BETTANY
ADAM GOLDBERG    JUDD HIRSCH    JOSH LUCAS    ANTHONY RAPP
and CHRISTOPHER PLUMMER    AUSTIN PENDLETON    JASON GRAY-STANFORD

| | | |
|---|---|---|
| Director of Photography<br>ROGER DEAKINS, A.S.C., B.S.C. | Music Composed by<br>JAMES HORNER | Based on the Book by<br>SYLVIA NASAR |
| Production Designer<br>WYNN THOMAS | "ALL LOVE CAN BE"<br>Music by JAMES HORNER | Co-Producer<br>MAUREEN PEYROT |
| Edited by<br>MIKE HILL • DAN HANLEY | Lyric by WILL JENNINGS<br>Vocals Performed by<br>CHARLOTTE CHURCH | Associate Producers<br>ALDRIC LA'AULI PORTER |
| Costume Designer<br>RITA RYACK | Casting by<br>JANE JENKINS, C.S.A.<br>JANET HIRSHENSON, C.S.A. | A BRIAN GRAZER Production<br>A RON HOWARD Film |

## CAST

| | |
|---|---|
| John Nash . . . . . . . . . . . . . . . . . RUSSELL CROWE | White-Haired Patient . . . . . . . . . RANCE HOWARD |
| Parcher . . . . . . . . . . . . . . . . . . . ED HARRIS | Code-Red Nurse . . . . . . . . . . . . . . . JJ CHABACK |
| Alicia Nash . . . . . . . . . . . . JENNIFER CONNELLY | Adjunct . . . . . . . . . . . . . . . . . . DARIUS STONE |
| Dr. Rosen . . . . . . . . . CHRISTOPHER PLUMMER | Princeton Professor . . . . . . . . . . . . . . JOSH PAIS |
| Charles . . . . . . . . . . . . . . . . . PAUL BETTANY | Toby . . . . . . . . . . . . . . . . . . . ALEX TOMA |
| Sol . . . . . . . . . . . . . . . . . . ADAM GOLDBERG | Joyce . . . . . . . . . . . . . VALENTINA CARDINALLI |
| Hansen . . . . . . . . . . . . . . . . . . JOSH LUCAS | Young Professor . . . . . . . . . . . TEAGLE F. BOUGERE |
| Bender . . . . . . . . . . . . . . . ANTHONY RAPP | John Nash, Jr. (Teenager) . . . . . . . . . DAVID B. ALLEN |
| Ainsley . . . . . . . . . . JASON GRAY-STANFORD | John Nash, Jr. (Young Man) . . . . . . . MICHAEL ESPER |
| Helinger . . . . . . . . . . . . . . . . . JUDD HIRSCH | Girl at Bar . . . . . . . . . CATHARINA EVA BURKLEY |
| Thomas King . . . . . . . . . . . AUSTIN PENDLETON | Blond in Bar . . . . . . . . . . . . . . . . . AMY WALZ |
| Marcee . . . . . . . . . . . . . . . VIVIEN CARDONE | Brunettes . . . . . . . . . . . . . TRACEY TOOMEY |
| Bar Co-ed . . . . . . . . . . . . . . . JILL M. SIMON | JENNIFER WEEDON |
| Professor Horner . . . . . . . . . . VICTOR STEINBACH | YVONNE THOMAS |
| Becky . . . . . . . . . . . . . . . . TANYA CLARKE | HOLLY PITRAGO |
| Captain . . . . . . . . . . . . . . . THOMAS F. WALSH | Pen Ceremony Professors . . . . . . ISADORE ROSENFELD |
| General . . . . . . . . . . . . . . . . . JESSE DORAN | THOMAS C. ALLEN |
| Analyst . . . . . . . . . . . . . . . . . KENT CASSELLA | DAVE BAYER |
| MIT Student . . . . . . . . . . PATRICK BLINDAUER | BRIAN KEITH LEWIS |
| Photographer . . . . . . . . . . . . . JOHN BLAYLOCK | TOM MCNUTT |
| Governor . . . . . . . . . . . . . . . . . ROY THINNES | WILL DUNHAM |
| Young Man . . . . . . . . . . . . ANTHONY EASTON | GLENN ROBERTS |
| Harvard Administrator . . . . . . . . CHERYL HOWARD | ED JUPP |

| | | |
|---|---|---|
| Princeton Students . . . . . | CHRISTOPHER STOCKTON | |
| | GREGORY DRESS | |
| | CARLA OCCHIOGROSSO | |
| | MATT SAMSON | |
| | LYENA NOMURA | |
| Insulin Treatment Nurses . . . . . | KATHLEEN FELLEGARA | |
| | BETSY KLOMPUS | |
| Technicians . . . . . . . . . . . . . . . | STELIO SAVANTE | |
| | LOGAN MCCALL | |
| | BOB BRODER | |

Stunt Coordinator . . . . . . . . . . . . PETER BUCOSSI
Additional Stunt Coordinator . . . . . . . . MIKE RUSSO
Stunts . . . . . . . . . . . . . . . . . . . TIM GALLIN

| | |
|---|---|
| JACK MCLAUGHLIN | PHIL RUDOLPH |
| DON HEWITT | JOHN RONEY |
| FRANK FERRARA | MICK O'ROURKE |
| BILL ANAGNOS | CHARLES PAGE |
| STEVE MACK | BRENNAN MCKAY |
| PAUL BUCOSSI | STEVEN POPE |
| BRIAN SMYJ | KEITH SIGLINGER |
| JAY BORYEA | |

Unit Production Manager
KATHLEEN MCGILL

First Assistant Director
ALDRIC LA'AULI PORTER

Second Assistant Director
KRISTEN BERNSTEIN

Re-Recording Mixers . . . . . . . . . . . CHRIS JENKINS
FRANK MONTAÑO (J.B.M.)

Art Director . . . . . . . . . . . . . . . ROBERT GUERRA
Asst. Art Directors . . . . . . . . . . . NANCY WINTERS
BRADLEY MAYER
Set Decorator . . . . . . . . . . . . . . . LESLIE ROLLINS
Asst. Set Decorator . . . . . . . . CHRISTINE MOOSHER
Property Master . . . . . . . . . . . . . . . . TOM ALLEN
Assistant Property Masters . . . . . . . BETSY KLOMPUS
ANN EDGEWORTH
Leadman . . . . . . . . . . . . . . . . . . . JOE PROSCIA
Camera Operator . . . . . . . . . . . . . KYLE RUDOLPH
First Assistant Camera . . . . . . . . . . . ANDY HARRIS
Second Assistant Camera . . . . . . . . PATRICK QUINN
B Camera Operator . . . . . . . . . . GERARDO PUGLIA
1st Assistant B Camera . . . . . . . . . . . TIM NORMAN
Camera Loader . . . . . . . . GABRIEL GOODENOUGH
Script Supervisor . . . . . . . . . . . . EVA Z. CABRERA
Dialect Coach . . . . . . . . . . . . . JUDI DICKERSON
Production Sound Mixer . . . . . . . . . . ALLAN BYER
Boom Operator . . . . . . . . . . . PATRICIA BROLSMA
Cableman . . . . . . . . . . . . . . . . ALFREDO VITERI
1st Assistant Editor . . . . . . RICHARD FRIEDLANDER
Assistant Editors . . . . . . . . . . . . . . GUY BARRESI
GLENN ALLEN
Apprentice Editor . . . . . . . . . . . . . . KATE EALES
Gaffer . . . . . . . . . . . . . . . . . WILLIAM O'LEARY
Best Boy Electric . . . . . . . . . . . . . JOE GRIMALDI
Electrics . . . . . . . . . . . . . . . . JEREMY KNASTER

| | |
|---|---|
| CHRIS ROSEN | MICHAEL MAURER |
| ED COHEN | DENNIS PETERS |

| | |
|---|---|
| RAY PREZIOSI | FRED MULLER |
| MIKE RUDOLPH | |

Rigging Gaffer . . . . . . . . . . . . . . . . RICH FORD
Rigging Best Boy Electric . . . . . . . LOUIS PETRAGLIA
Rigging Electrics . . . . . . . . . . . . LANCE SHEPARD
JIM GALVIN
GEORGE HINES
BRIAN MURPHY
Key Grip . . . . . . . . . . . . . . . . . MITCH LILLIAN
Best Boy Grip . . . . . . . . . CHARLIE MARROQUIN
Dolly Grips . . . . . . . . . . . . . . . BRUCE HAMME
RICK MARROQUIN
Grips . . . . . . . . . . . . . . . . . . PAUL CANDRILLI

| | |
|---|---|
| FRANZ YEICH | ANDY SWEENEY |
| TED ROBINSON | CHRIS VACCARO |
| THOMAS MCGRATH WOODS | |

Key Rigging Grip . . . . . . . . . . . . . JIM BONIECE
Best Boy Rigging Grip . . . . . . . . MIKE MCFADDEN
Rigging Grips . . . . . . . . . . . HOWARD DAVIDSON
TODD KLEIN
Special Effects Coordinator . . . . . . . . . WILL CABAN
Special Effects . . . . . . . . . . . . . STEVE KIRSHOFF
Special Effects Assistants . . . . . . . . . . FRED KRAMER
GILBERT GERTSEN
Asst. Costume Designer . . . . . . . . KEVIN BRAINERD
Costume Supervisors . . . . . . . . . . . BILL CAMPBELL
WINSOME G. MCKOY
Mr. Crowe's Costumer . . . . . . . . . . . PETER WHITE
Wardrobe Assistant . . . . . . . . . . . . . M.J. MCGRATH
Seamstress . . . . . . . . . . . . . . . LAURIE BUEHLER
Key Hair Stylist . . . . . . . . . . COLLEEN CALLAGHAN
Hair Stylists . . . . . . . . . . . . . . . . DALE BROWNELL
SUZY MAZZARESE ALLISON
Makeup Dept. Head . . . . . . . . . . . . . NEAL MARTZ
Key Makeup . . . . . . . . . . . . . . TODD KLEITSCH
Ms. Connelly's Makeup . . . . . KYMBRA CALLAGHAN
Makeup Artist . . . . . . . . . . . . . . . . LINDA LAZAR
Location Manager . . . . . . . . . . . . LYN PINEZICH
Assistant Location Managers . . . . . . . . MIKE KRIARIS

| | |
|---|---|
| PATTY CAREY | CHRIS GEORGE |
| NICOLE KLETT | RANDY MANION |
| JASON FARRAR | |

Production Accountant . . . . . . . . . . . TAMARA BALLY
Asst. Unit Production Manager . . . . . . LORI JOHNSON
Production Coordinator . . . . . . . . . . DAVID BAUSCH
2nd 2nd Assistant Director . . . . NOREEN R. CHELEDEN
DGA Trainee . . . . . . . . . . . . . . JANE FERGUSON
1st Assistant Accountant . . . . . . . . . . JUDY PURSELY
2nd Assistant Accountant . . . . . . . STEVE GINSBURG
Payroll Accountant . . . . . . . . . . . . MACALL POLAY
Construction Accountant . . . . . . . JEREMY D. PRATT
Accounting Clerk . . . . . . . . . . . TONY HERNANDEZ
Casting Assistant . . . . . . . . . . . KRISTIN MCTIGUE
Extras Casting . . . . . . . . . . BILL DANCE CASTING
Extras Casting Associate . . . WENDY GOODMAN THUM
Unit Publicist . . . . . . . . . . . . . JULIE KUEHNDORF
Still Photographer . . . . . . . . . . . . . . . ELI REED
Assistant to Mr. Hallowell . . . . . . . . EVA BURKLEY
Assistant to Mr. Grazer . . . . . . . . . . . ANNA CULP
Assistants to Mr. Crowe . . . . . . . . MARK DUMBRELL
MEREDITH GARLICK

| | |
|---|---|
| Mr. Crowe's Trainer . . . . . . . . LOURENE BEVAART | |
| Art Dept. Administrator . . . . . . . . . . . ERIK KNIGHT | |
| Asst. Production Coordinator . . . . . JANE KELLY KOSEK | |
| Production Secretaries. . . . . . . MICHELLE MACIRELLA | |
| | AUDRA POLK |
| Production Assistants. . . . . . . . . . . JOHN SILVESTRI | |
| CHRIS COLLINS | MIKKI ZISKA |
| GARY S. RAKE | MELISSA BRIDES |
| SHAWN ALEXANDER | DAVID CATALANO |
| MEHGAN PORTER | DAVID TOMASINI |
| RACHEL MAY | KEVIN WILLIAMS |
| KIMIE KIMURA-HEANE | AARON DUNSAY |
| TOM GRAVEL | GANIOUS |
| MARIANNE BELL | TARA MUSKUS |
| BRIAN LENNON | |
| Storyboard Artists . . . . . . . . . . . . . BRICK MASON | |
| | WARREN DRUMMOND |
| Graphic Artist . . . . . . . . . . . . . . . . LEO HOLDER | |
| Projectionist . . . . . . . . . . . . EDMUND NARDONE | |
| Construction Coordinator . . . . . MARTIN BERNSTEIN | |
| Key Carpenter Foreman . . RICHARD BRYAN DOUGLAS | |
| Key Construction Grip . . . . . . . . . . . ARNE OLSEN | |
| Charge Scenic . . . . . . . . . . . . . . . JEFF GLAVE | |
| Transportation Captain . . . . . . . . . . . . MIKE HYDE | |
| Transportation Co-Captain . . . . . . ROBERT BUCKMAN | |
| Craft Service. . . . . . . . . . . . . . . . JEANNE JIRIK | |

## SECOND UNIT

| | |
|---|---|
| 2nd Unit Director . . . . . . . . . . TODD HALLOWELL | |
| 1st Assistant Director . . . . . . . . . . . . . JOE BURNS | |
| 2nd Assistant Director . . . . . . . . . . . SHEA ROWAN | |
| Director of Photography . . . . . . . . . DAVE DUNLAP | |
| Gaffer. . . . . . . . . . . . . . . . . GREG ADDISON | |
| Best Boy Electric . . . . . . . . . . . . . PETER WALTS | |
| Electrics . . . . . . . . . . . . . . . . . SAM FRIEDMAN | |
| | JEFF KEATON |
| Key Grip . . . . . . . . . . . . . . . . . SAL LANZA | |
| Best Boy Grip . . . . . . . . . . . JON NUSSBAUM | |
| Dolly Grip. . . . . . . . . . . . . . . KEN FUNDUS | |
| Grips . . . . . . . . . . . . . . . . . GLEN WEINSTEIN | |
| | KEITH KASTNER |
| | JOHN HALLIGAN |
| | ANDREW FARLEY |
| 1st Assistant Camera . . . . . . . . . . . . . JIM BELLETIER | |
| 2nd Assistant Camera . . . . . . . . . . . . . KRIS ENOS | |
| Sound Mixer. . . . . . . . . . . . . . TONY STARBUCK | |
| Boom Operator . . . . . . . . . JOEL ROI ARONOWITZ | |
| Costume Supervisors . . . . . . . . . . . MARCIA OSTE | |
| | KEVIN DRAVES |
| Key Hair Stylist. . . . . . . . . . . ANTOINETTE CARR | |
| Key Makeup . . . . . . . . . . . . . . . DENNIS EGER | |
| Property Master. . . . . . . . . . . PAUL WEATHERED | |
| Assistant Props . . . . . . . . . . . . . . TYLER KIM | |
| Script Supervisor . . . . . . . . . LYNNE TWENTYMAN | |
| Location Manager . . . . . . . . . . . EVAN PERAZZO | |
| Standby Set Dresser . . . . . . . . ANTHONY MUNAFO | |
| Transportation Captain. . . . . . . . JAMES MCGRANE | |
| Video Assist . . . . . . . . . . . . . . GREG EDWARDS | |
| Production Assistants . . . . . . . . . STEVEN GORDON | |
| JASON KADLEC | DARREN MAYNARD |

| | |
|---|---|
| CAT BURKLEY | YOON KIM |
| Post Production Supervisor. . . . . STEVE CASTELLANO | |
| Supervising Sound Editor . . . . . . CHIC CICCOLINI III | |
| Dialogue Editors. . . . . . . . . . . . . STAN BOCHNER | |
| | LOU CERBORINO |
| | MARC LAUB |
| ADR Supervisor. . . . . . . . . . DEBORAH WALLACH | |
| ADR Assistant Editor . . . . . . . KENNA DOERINGER | |
| Sound Effects Editors . . . . . . . . HARRY PECK BOLLES | |
| | EYTAN MIRSKY |
| | DANIEL PAGAN |
| Foley Editors . . . . . . . . . . . . . . MISSY COHEN | |
| | PATRICK DUNDAS |
| Assistant Sound Editor . . . . . . . . . . DON PEEBLES | |
| Post Production Assistant. . . . . . . NICOLE MACAGNA | |
| Recordist . . . . . . . . . . . . . . . . ROBERT OLARI | |
| ADR Mixers . . . . . . . . . . . . . . . PAUL ZYDEL | |
| | DEAN DRABIN |
| | MICHAEL THOMPSON |
| ADR Recordists. . . . . . . . . . . . . DOUG MURRAY | |
| | CLAUDIA CARLE |
| | LIVIA RUZIC |
| Loop Group Coordinator . . . . . . . LYNNE REDDING | |
| Foley Artists . . . . . . . . . . . . . . NANCY CABRERA | |
| | GINGER GEARY |
| Foley Recording Studio . . . . . . . . . . . . . C5, INC. | |
| Music Editor. . . . . . . . . . . . . . JIM HENRIKSON | |
| Assistant Music Editor . . . . . BARBARA MCDERMOTT | |
| Executive in Charge of Film Music for Universal Studios | |
| | KATHY NELSON |
| Music Supervisor . . . . . . . . . JULYCE MONBLEAUX | |
| Music Scoring Mixer . . . . . . . . . . SIMON RHODES | |
| Orchestrations . . . . . . . . . . . . JAMES HORNER | |
| | RANDY KERBER |
| Music Preparation . . . . . . . . . . . BOB BORNSTEIN | |
| Music Contractor . . . . . . . . SANDY DECRESCENT | |
| Music Recorded & Mixed at . . . TODD SCORING STAGE | |
| Studio Manager . . . . . . . . . . . KIRSTEN SMITH | |
| Dermatologist. . . . . . . . . . DAVID COLBERT, M.D. | |
| Set Medics. . . . . . . . . . KATHY & RICH FELLEGARA | |
| Psychology Consultant . . . . . DR. MARIANNE GILLOW | |
| Math Consultant . . . . . . . . . . . . . DAVE BAYER | |
| Princeton Consultant . . . . . . . . . . HAROLD KU`HN | |
| Video Assist . . . . . . . . . . . . . KEVIN MCKENNA | |
| Catering . . . . . . . . . . . . . . . . . . TOMKATS | |
| Titles and Opticals . . . . . . . . . . . PACIFIC TITLE | |
| Negative Cutter . . . . . . . . . . . . GARY BURRITT | |
| Color Timer . . . . . . . . . . . . . . MIKE MILLIKAN | |
| Lighting . . . . . . . . . . CAMERA SERVICE CENTER | |
| Arriflex 535 Cameras. . . . . . . . . . . OTTO NEMENZ | |

Special Visual Effects and Digital Animation
DIGITAL DOMAIN

| | |
|---|---|
| Visual Effects Supervisor. . . . . . . . . . . KEVIN MACK | |
| Visual Effects Producer. . . . . . . . KELLY L'ESTRANGE | |
| Digital Effects Supervisor . . . . . . MATTHEW BUTLER | |
| Compositing Supervisor . . . . . . . . . CLAAS HENKE | |
| 3D Integration Lead. . . . . . . . . . . SWEN GILLBERG | |
| 3D Integration Artists. . . . . . . . . . NANCY ADAMS | |
| JASON DOSS | SCOTT EDELSTEIN |
| CHRIS LOGAN | |